The Book of Scams

Every owner of a physical copy of this edition of

The Book of Scams

can download the eBook for free direct from us at Harriman House, in a DRM-free format that can be read on any eReader, tablet or smartphone.

Simply head to:

ebooks.harriman-house.com/bookofscams

to get your copy now.

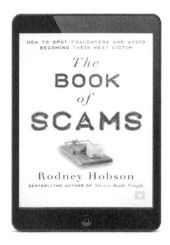

THE BOOK OF SCAMS

How to spot fraudsters and avoid becoming their next victim

Rodney Hobson

Hh

HARRIMAN HOUSE LTD
18 College Street
Petersfield
Hampshire
GU31 4AD
GREAT BRITAIN
Tel: +44 (0)1730 233870
Email: enquiries@harriman-house.com
Website: www.harriman-house.com

First published in Great Britain in 2016
Copyright © Rodney Hobson

The right of Rodney Hobson to be identified as the author has been asserted in accordance with the Copyright, Design and Patents Act 1988.

Print ISBN: 978-0-85719-486-2
eBook ISBN: 978-0-85719-515-9

British Library Cataloguing in Publication Data
A CIP catalogue record for this book can be obtained from the British Library.

Whilst every effort has been made to ensure that information in this book is accurate, no liability can be accepted for any loss incurred in any way whatsoever by any person relying solely on the information contained herein.

No responsibility for loss occasioned to any person or corporate body acting or refraining to act as a result of reading material in this book can be accepted by the Publisher, by the Author, or by the employers of the Author.

CONTENTS

ABOUT THE AUTHOR

Rodney Hobson is an experienced financial journalist who has held senior editorial positions with publications in the UK and Asia.

Among posts he has held are News Editor for the Business section of the *Times*, Business Editor of the *Singapore Monitor*, Deputy Business Editor of the *Far Eastern Economic Review*, Head of News at Citywire and Editor of *Shares* magazine. He has also contributed to the *Daily Mail*, the *Independent* and *Business Franchise Magazine*. He is registered as a Representative with the Financial Conduct Authority.

He writes a weekly investment column for the Morningstar financial website, makes guest appearances on Share Radio, speaks at investment conferences and delivers guest lectures on cruise ships.

Rodney is married with one daughter.

Also by Rodney Hobson

Investing titles

Shares Made Simple
Small Companies, Big Profits
Understanding Company News
How to Build a Share Portfolio
The Dividend Investor

Paul Amos detective stories

Dead Money
Unlikely Graves
Holy Murder
Kith and Kill

PREFACE

Who this book is for

Everybody has been approached by a scammer at some point in their lives, or knows someone who has. When I give talks on financial scams I am beset with accounts from those present who want to tell me about their experiences in either falling for or thwarting a fraudster.

Modern communications and rising living standards have greatly encouraged financial fraud, making it easier and more worthwhile to target a wide range of people. Fraudsters do not need to con everyone they target: just a small proportion of potential victims can produce a lucrative income.

Danger lurks for those unwary souls who part too readily with their hard-earned cash. *The Book of Scams* will help you be alert to the risks. You will learn how to spot scams and avoid falling for them while, dare one say it, reaching an understanding of the sheer nerve and resourcefulness of many scammers.

It is also meant to entertain, as we learn to grudgingly admire as well as despise these ingenious crooks.

How this book is structured

Rather than simply relating scams in a higgledy-piggledy fashion or listing them according to when they first occurred, I have made what I believe is the first serious attempt to identify the types of scams that are perpetrated and arrange them by their characteristics.

This makes the basic principles behind each type of scam more recognisable and it shows how scams have evolved and re-emerged through time. Many scams fall into more than one category, but I have grouped them according to what is most appropriate.

In Section A, I look at the ingredients of a scam, the perpetrators and the victims. I then look at traditional scams dating right back to the first book of the Bible and running through to the era of imaginative scams in the 1920s. This *golden age* saw the birth of the Ponzi scheme, perhaps the most famous type of scam ever devised.

In Section B, I consider investment scams, from the early days of stock market scandals when the London Stock Exchange was in its infancy, through to the present day boiler rooms and cold callers.

In Section C, I move on to the latest golden age of scams based on modern technology, most notably the internet. It is clear that no one is safe from the attentions of the scammers, but I will show how a modicum of common sense and awareness can thwart even the most persistent fraudsters.

The line between what is legal but of dubious morality and what is downright fraud can be very thin. I shall distinguish between the two sides of the moral and legal code as far as is practical.

Throughout the book I will normally refer to the fraudster as he, simply because the overwhelming majority of them are male. However, when used in a general sense you should take 'he' to mean 'he or she'.

INTRODUCTION

I RECEIVED A TELEPHONE CALL FROM A MAN WHO CLAIMED TO be in the fraud department of my bank.

My card had been cloned, he said, and was being used fraudulently in shops in Oxford Street. He actually named a couple of well-known retailers there. My wife and I were both at home and both had our cards in our possession.

It could have been a genuine call. On a previous occasion my card had been cloned and the fake was being used in America, which alerted my bank's fraud department and they called to let me know. That call had been legitimate, but I had treated it initially with a suspicion that had bordered on rudeness.

So I played the caller along this time, taking care not to give away any useful information, until I was satisfied that he was a scammer. He overplayed his hand, asking what other credit cards I had.

When he claimed within seconds that he had contacted the issuers and they had stopped the other cards I knew for certain this was a trick. It was just not possible to do so without the card numbers and without the other bank speaking directly to me.

I kept the call going until we reached the point where he wanted to send a courier to my house to collect my card for analysis. Not likely.

When I told him I was a finance writer who exposed this kind of scam he let off a stream of words that I have never heard a bank employee use. Nor, to the best of my knowledge, do bank managers threaten to send round the boys with guns to kill even the most uncooperative of account holders.

There are some lessons we can learn immediately:

- Scammers often adopt an air of authority to try to gain the upper hand

- They tend to have well prepared scripts

- If you keep them talking you may be able to see flaws in their stories

- Never panic if you are approached, but try to think clearly

This book looks at scams ancient and modern, from the hilarious to the scary, to show how scams work, how scammers think and how you can spot when you are being had.

Do not assume that you are too clever to fall for a scam. Fraudsters can be remarkably persuasive and they are forever refining old scams or devising new ones. Intelligent and successful people have been taken in. This book will help you to be on your guard and avoid becoming the next victim.

SECTION A.
TRADITIONAL SCAMS

CHAPTER 1.
The Ingredients
Of A Scam

What is a scam?

THE DICTIONARY DEFINES A SCAM AS A FRAUDULENT
scheme; a swindle. The word also exists as a verb, meaning
to cheat; to defraud.

A scam involves persuading someone to part with money in
return for goods or services that are not needed, or provided to
a very poor standard. As in the example in the Introduction,
scams also involve attempts to steal financial or other personal
information from victims. The fraudster then usually disappears
or is uncontactable.

There is a very thin line between what constitutes a scam
and what is merely sharp practice. One may argue over

whether the fixing of interest and foreign exchange rates by banks constitutes a scam, but the point is that banks at least come under a regulatory authority that can force them to refund their victims. You can also take your business elsewhere if you are dissatisfied. True scams are deliberate frauds that are outside any regulatory framework.

When it comes to financial scams, remember the duck theory. If it looks like a duck, quacks like a duck and swims like a duck, it's probably a duck. If it looks like a scam, sounds like a scam and smells like a scam, it's probably a scam.

Financial scams have been around for as long as there have been people with assets and others who covet those assets; for as long as there have been haves and have-nots; for as long as some have been willing to work for a living and others who would rather sponge off them.

While different scams work in different ways, there are certain characteristics shared by scammers and their victims.

Scammers are:
- Cunning
- Determined
- Persistent
- Highly plausible
- Utterly lacking in conscience
- Opportunistic

Victims are:
- Naïve
- Gullible
- Trusting
- Lonely

- Greedy
- Easily worn down

These characteristics do not all apply to every fraudster or every victim. They are a broad brush summing up the people on both sides of a successful scam.

You'll notice I haven't included 'stupid' in the list of victims' traits; do not assume that they are. Many intelligent people have been caught out by a plausible scammer.

The golden ages of scams

Scams tend to run in cycles. The first golden age came around the turn of the 18th century when share dealing and world trade were in their infancy and investors were lured into weird and wonderful notions of making fortunes from projects in far away places they knew nothing about.

The 1920s was the second golden age of scams, helped in part by the social turmoil that followed the first world war. It saw the birth of one of the most famous types of recurring fraud, the Ponzi scheme, which we will analyse in a later chapter, and some spectacular 'sales' of popular landmarks that leave you with a sneaking admiration for the sheer nerve and imagination of the perpetrators.

The third golden age is now with us. Modern communications have opened up a whole array of weapons for scammers, while prosperity has provided more potential victims with money to be parted from.

Scams often rely on the latest technology or social phenomenon to gain a new lease of life. While the technology changes, the scams reappear in much the same form through history, although in a different disguise. Thus we will see recurring themes as we learn more about the scams. This leads us to the important lesson that although methods change, a scam is a scam and its hallmarks can be spotted in any era.

By grasping the underlying principles, we give ourselves the best chance of spotting a scam when it is staring us in the face.

Let us now move on to the types of scam that follow the most basic rules of how to part vulnerable victims from their cash – what I have called the Traditional Scams.

CHAPTER 2.

The Kick 'Em When They're Down Scam

THE ANGELS TELL US NEVER TO KICK SOMEONE WHEN they're down. It's not very sporting. The devil says that's when to kick them, because they can't kick you back.

Scammers are like vicious muggers. They knock you to the ground and carry on kicking you until you hand over everything they can take.

Such scams are usually perpetrated through a knock on the door or by persistent phone calls. They generally target the elderly, who are:

- More trusting
- More easily frightened
- More likely to become befuddled
- Less likely to remember details

- Less likely to ask for credentials
- Less likely to complain

They typically involve persuading householders that urgent repairs are needed and/or that they need to draw money out of their accounts and hand it over.

Elderly victim of fake detectives

Among reports of preying on the vulnerable was the story of an elderly woman approached at home by two men who claimed to be detectives. They told her that the local branch of Barclays, where she banked, was staffed by fraudsters who would take all her money.

They persuaded the victim to help with a plan that would supposedly trap the crooked bank staff. She was to go to the branch and draw out a large sum of money. Since the bank staff were crooked, this cash would be counterfeit and therefore the woman would not be able to spend it.

Instead, she was to hand it to the 'detectives' waiting outside who would then use the counterfeit money as evidence. The money was counterfeit, so the sum would not be deducted from her account.

It must be said in fairness to Barclays Bank staff that there was not a jot of truth in this story, nor was there any suggestion that any member of staff was involved in the con.

One can see immediately why the conmen needed to find someone trusting and not worldly wise, someone who could be easily badgered into doing as she was instructed, who would not ask for proof that they were detectives. The story is full of holes, as cons often are if you look at them carefully:

- If the police knew there was counterfeit money in the branch, why didn't they just go in and confiscate it?

- Would the police really involve an elderly member of the public in exposing the supposed scam?
- Why did they not use a police officer or employee from another bank branch to pose as a customer?
- Why was this matter not being handled by the fraud squad?
- How was the woman going to be reimbursed for the withdrawal from her account?

Any member of the public is entitled to ask a person claiming to be a police officer to produce his or her warrant card. You can ask what police station they are based at and ring to see if they are genuine – making sure that they remain outside your locked front door while you do so. Do not allow them access to your home.

Better still is to suggest that the 'police officer' finds someone else to do their dirty work. If you receive such an approach, report it to the real police.

Targeting vulnerable people may be done at the door or on the phone and fraudsters will often keep hammering away until the victim is worn down. The trouble is that if you give way once they will come back time and time again, like blackmailers, as we shall see in the next chapter.

If you think you are vulnerable to fraudsters, never allow yourself to be rushed into taking action you may later regret.

The dating scam

We tend to think of the elderly as being vulnerable, but none are so vulnerable as those who are lonely and looking for love in all the wrong places.

Tales of both sexes falling for utter cads and being taken to the cleaners are as old as any in the scamming chronicles, but preying on the feelings of hapless prospective partners has been given an extra boost by online dating.

Dating agencies and websites may be above board in themselves, but no one can vouch for those who register.

As with so many scams, no one can say with any degree of certainty how many people are duped by bogus lovers because victims are often too embarrassed to complain or they see no point in doing so. The *Sunday Times* reported that one woman, a 61-year-old health worker who was looking after dementia sufferers – so she was hardly naïve or unintelligent – fell victim to a scammer on an online dating site who claimed to be a high flier with an American toy firm.

He managed to convince her to hand over £200 for medical treatment, though a high flier would surely be able to find £200 of his own money. She got off lightly. Other lovelorn innocents have been taken for far more.

It is hard to advise lovers that they should let their heads rule their hearts, but blind dates do involve meeting strangers about whom you know nothing except what they themselves have put on the website. The further away from you that they live, the easier it is for them to disappear, especially if they come from or live overseas.

In particular, if you find yourself in this situation you should be very wary of a partner who asks for money. Worse still is a date who needs cash but says they wouldn't dream of taking it off you. In this situation you are being softened up so that you may insist on paying.

If you feel you really must do the decent thing, at least insist on handing the money over directly to wherever it is supposed to be going, such as a medical centre that is supposedly providing the treatment for example.

If the money is to clear debts, resist the temptation. It won't solve anything because clearing the debt does not address what got someone into debt in the first place. In these situations debts are generally amassed as a result of an addiction, such as gambling or shopping. Clearing an existing debt provides funds to fuel the addiction. Alternatively, your lover may use the money to do a runner, away from the clutches of creditors.

If you use dating sites, follow these rules in assessing a potential date:

- Don't hand over money. If you never hear from the date again you know he or she was only interested in your money.

- If you find yourself incurring unexpected costs you are being taken for a mug.

- Be wary if your date seems to be in too much of a hurry to find out confidential information about you.

- Be particularly wary if your date is keen to establish your financial status.

Inheritance scams

Where there's a will there's relations and it seems that blood is not always thicker than water. Unfortunately there is no such thing as a watertight will, even one that is drawn up by a solicitor.

As we get older we unfortunately tend to become more vulnerable and more lonely, and thus more susceptible to scams that prey on those least able to resist. That unhappy situation is compounded when we are ill, frail or dying.

A fair proportion of those drawing up or finalising their will are elderly, which means they are vulnerable and open to manipulation. In such areas it is hard to draw a line between taking advantage and outright fraud.

The first scam in recorded history is a prime example of *kick 'em when they're down*. There are lessons to be learnt several thousand years later.

The earliest scam in recorded history

Dates in the Bible are a little hazy but the Old Testament has its fair share of unpleasant characters and it seems likely that the earliest recorded financial scam can be found in *Genesis*, the first book of the Old Testament, in chapters 25 and 27. It is a classic story of kicking not one but two men when they are too weak to fight back.

Isaac and Rebekah were parents of twin brothers, Esau and Jacob, who were born so close together that Jacob was holding Esau's heel. Alas, there were no prizes for second place, however close the race. Esau was the first born and therefore under the prevailing custom was entitled to his father's blessing and the entire inheritance.

The two brothers rapidly grew apart. Esau was a hunter and the apple of his father's eye; Jacob was a farmer and a mummy's boy. They were said to have fought in the womb and there was little brotherly love outside it.

He sold his birthright for a mess of pottage

One day Esau came home from hunting utterly exhausted. Tired and starving, he begged Jacob for a mess of pottage, which posh readers may call a casserole and others will know as a bowl of stew.

Jacob demanded that in return Esau relinquish his inheritance to him. Jacob was persistent, without conscience; Esau was vulnerable and easily worn down. Fearing that he would die anyway without food, Esau sold his birthright for a mess of pottage.

It is just about possible to argue that this was a bargain struck between a willing buyer and a willing seller, that there is nothing immoral in striking a hard bargain. What followed, however, was downright disgraceful.

Smooth and hairy

As Isaac lay blind and dying, he asked Esau to go out on a hunting expedition to shoot a deer and prepare a dish of venison, which he so enjoyed. Rebekah overheard the plan and while Esau was away she summoned Jacob to kill a couple of young goats so she could prepare a substitute meal. Jacob would pretend to be his older brother and would present the meal to his father. Blind Isaac would then give him his blessing – and formally hand over the inheritance.

With relish that would have done Lady Macbeth proud, Rebekah now demonstrated two essential ingredients of a successful scam: plan carefully and hold your nerve. She was made of sterner stuff than Jacob, who started whingeing about getting caught out, saying: "My brother Esau is a hairy man and I am smooth." Supposing Isaac touched him?

Rebekah had thought of that. She chopped the skin off the goats and wrapped one piece round Jacob's arm and another round his neck.

Isaac was indeed suspicious, saying words to the effect of: "You got back a bit smartish, didn't you?" He also recognised Jacob's voice.

Believing what you want to believe

However, as so often with victims of scams, Isaac believed what he wanted to believe, that this really was Esau. So when he touched Jacob's kid-lined skin and felt it was hairy he swallowed the bait along with the meat.

Isaac thus blessed the wrong son and made him the master of the household. The real Esau returned with venison only moments too late. Timing is often another important ingredient of scams. It is usually important to hurry the victim into the trap.

For those who like an element of justice with their bedtime stories, Esau was so narked that Jacob fled for his life, so no benefit came from the scheme after all.

You can't trust your own mother

Cheating your own family seems particularly cruel. One such story is that of Miss Denvar Bathie, whose father left £90,000 to be divided between his three children.

Miss Bathie put £20,000 aside to pay for her wedding and provide a deposit on a house. Her mother, Trudy Collins, suggested that Miss Bathie would fritter the money away and she persuaded her daughter to hand over her bank card and PIN for safe keeping.

Mrs Collins betrayed this trust by spending most of the money herself, on holidays, shopping trips, hotels and hairdressers. It was only when NatWest bank rang Miss Bathie to query some of the outgoings that she realised she had been betrayed by her own mother.

This is a warning that you can never wholly trust anyone else with your money, not even a close relation. The larger the sum of money, the greater the temptation.

Contesting a will

While some countries, such as France, have a set formula for who inherits what, British law is based on the principle that we can leave our money to who we want. As such, we do not have the automatic right to any inheritance.

Thus it is difficult to contest a will other than by arguing that the will is unclear; the testator – the person making the will – was not in his or her right mind; or the beneficiaries exerted undue pressure to get the will drawn up in their favour. While the first reason is a matter of fact, the other two are difficult to prove.

If you do feel that jiggery pokery has taken place you can challenge a will on the grounds of validity. Alternatively you can claim undue influence, which involves providing compelling evidence of coercion rather than just moderate persuasion. It may also be possible to claim that the testator did not fully understand or approve of the contents.

However, challenging a will can cost a lot in time, money and your health, and it is rare for wills to be overturned in court. Win or lose, you will be generating a good deal of ill will and bitterness.

Forged wills

Proving that a will has been forged is also problematic, but generally easier. At least there is tangible evidence in the form of three signatures – that of the perpetrator plus two witnesses.

The perpetrators are motivated by greed and will often let this get the better of them. That is how Dr Shipman, the notorious GP from Hyde, who was killing off elderly patients, gave himself away. He forged one will too many.

A Birmingham woman who forged her partner's will was caught selling his possessions on eBay. She had left her husband and moved in with another man, who then died of cancer. She forged a will for the new partner with the help of her ex-husband.

The deceased had run a car refurbishment business and he and the woman, who he met after her divorce, bought a house, a canal boat and expensive cars. No doubt she got to enjoy the lifestyle and she probably felt entitled to a share of the near £1 million estate, as she had put some of her own money into the business and she also took over running the business and cared for him when he fell ill.

She told the dead man's grown up children that he had not made a will, then claimed that the estate had been left to her under the terms of a will which she forged. Her former husband provided two false witnesses and an executor.

The children became suspicious when they noticed their late father's possessions, including an old red phone box, dining tables, lawnmowers and electrical equipment, being sold on eBay. They queried the will and discovered that it was a forgery. The woman and her ex-husband were given suspended jail sentences.

How the kick 'em when they're down scam has changed over the years

While the basic scam of preying on the vulnerable has remained the same throughout the centuries, social factors have made this a more common occurrence:

- People are living longer and the rising incidence of dementia means that there are more vulnerable elderly people to prey on.

- The working population is more mobile so communities break down and families live further apart, which means there is less opportunity for us to look out for each other.

- The closure of churches, libraries and pubs, especially in rural areas, has removed a focal point for communities where lonely people can interact.

- The closure of small police stations removes an opportunity for those who suspect they are being conned to talk face to face with someone they can trust.

- In a wealthier society people have more savings and assets to be conned out of.

How we can beat the scammers

- It goes against the grain to say this, but we live in an age where we need to be less trusting and more cynical. In particular, we need to be suspicious when approached by complete strangers.

- Discuss any approach that will cost you money with someone you know and trust. Very few problems need to be dealt with on the spot so there is no harm in getting a second opinion. Do not be panicked into immediate action.

- Be wary of seemingly free advice. Someone usually ends up paying so make sure that person isn't you.

- Befriend any vulnerable person you know and tell them to contact you if they receive any unsolicited approach. Talking things over helps potential victims to see through scams.

The above advice applies to many scams and is worth bearing in mind as we move onto a popular recurring fraud, the Letter from Lagos, in the next chapter.

CHAPTER 3.
The Letter From Lagos Scam

T HERE'S AN OLD SAYING AMONG COMEDIANS THAT YOU don't need new jokes, just new audiences. Now that jokes can whizz round the internet, finding new audiences has never been harder.

You may think that the same applies to scams. They are widely publicised on the internet and in newspapers, as well as by word of mouth. Yet some old favourites keep coming round. The fact that the scammers think they are worth another go indicates that people still fall for them.

The classic is surely the letter from Lagos, so called because in earlier versions it purported to emanate from the Nigerian capital. It can, however, be linked to any country, preferably one with a dubious political regime and tight foreign currency controls.

The basic theme is that someone has money trapped in a country and your help is needed to get it out. You will be amply rewarded for your assistance. You are asked to provide the name of the bank, the name on the account, the sort code and your account number.

The money will be transferred into your account and you will subsequently be asked to transmit the money, minus your substantial percentage of the proceeds, on to another account, details of which will be supplied in due course.

In reality, the scammer uses the details you have helpfully provided to empty your bank account, not put money in.

Although the story can vary enormously, the different versions have common themes:

- **Loadsamoney.** We are talking hundreds of millions of dollars, possibly billions. Although you are offered only a percentage of the loot, it tends to be a decent percentage, certainly enough to make you an overnight multi-millionaire.

- **A tug on the heart strings.** It's a story of injustice, where you are supposedly helping right a wrong. Usually someone has died, possibly executed at the hands of a corrupt regime, and a destitute widow or orphans are desperately trying to get access to what is rightfully theirs.

- **Minimal effort.** All you have to do is provide details of your bank account and they do the rest. What could possibly go wrong?

- **YOU are the one who is being trusted**. Since the money is being transferred to your bank account, you gain access to their money. They are relying entirely on you to do the decent thing and pass the money on – minus the share that you are entitled to, of course.

- **OK, it's illegal.** Strictly speaking this is breaking the law but only in a foreign country, and usually one run by a corrupt regime at that. As long as we keep this between ourselves, no one will get into trouble.

The following example, attempting to play on political upheaval in Lebanon, purported to emanate from Beirut.

Private/Confidential

Attn: President / Managing Director.
From: Mrs. Nazek Audi Hariri.

Date: 06-Jan-07

Greetings to you, with warm heart I offer my friendship, and greetings, and I hope this fax meets you in good time. However strange or surprising this contact might seem to you as we have not met personally or had any dealings in the past, I humbly ask that you will take due consideration of its importance and the immense benefit it will be to you. After careful consideration with my children, we resolved to contact you for your most needed assistance in this manner I duly apologize for infringing in your privacy, if this contact is not acceptable to you, as I make this proposal to you as a matter of integrity. First and foremost I wish to introduce myself properly to you. My name is Mrs. Nazek Audi Hariri, mother of five, my husband Mr. Rafik Baha al-din Hariri a very successful businessman and proficient politician in Lebanon. Though I was involved in some of my husband's business, which was very vast and successful. My beloved husband was among those killed in the massive explosion that rocked central Beirut's fashionable seafront district, on his was back from Lebanon parliament on 14th February 2005. http://www.cnn.com/2005/world/meast/02/14/beirut.hariri/index.html

When my husband died, I was contacted as next of kin by a private security firm in Europe to come forth to claim the consignment with the Certificate of Deposit and claim a safety deposit my husband has in their vault in his name. I discovered a Certificate of Deposit for the safety deposit with this private security firm, and other documents relating to the safety deposit in a book. The safety deposit, which is a trunk, is stock with hard currency (US Dollars) totaling $86,000,000 (Eighty Six Million US Dollar), which was generated from cash payments from his business associates.

Like many of this genre, it is excessively wordy. The above is only the opening salvo. Also typical is that it helpfully provides a link to a story about a real explosion, on a genuine and reputable website, that happened early in 2005.

From the date at the top of the letter it seems that this particular scam started running two years later, but as often happens the scammer provided a clue for unwary recipients. He forgot to change the date as the years rolled by and was still sending out letters dated 6 January 2007 as late as the middle of 2014.

This next email is another typical example, though in this case Holland was chosen as the source of funds. Scammers are always willing to try a new twist.

LETTER FROM LOLLY STEVENS.

May I apologise for intruding into your privacy. My name is Lolly Stevens a citizen of Wales presently in England, My family and I are having problems getting our family funds (twenty million dollars) out of a security company in Holland, since the death of my father. We need your help to assist us and you will have a share of seven million dollars, but since we have not met before, I decided to seek your permission before going you the details. If you will be so kind enough to grant me the permission, I will be glad to give you the details. Thank you for your time and I will be waiting for your response. Please reply to me back at lollystevens@yahoo.com.hk

Thanks,

Lolly Stevens

There was a giveaway that should arouse the suspicions of any recipient: why was the email address a Hong Kong one? The sender is supposedly in either the Netherlands or the UK, neither of which is particularly inclined to block money that genuinely belongs to one of its bona fide residents.

The letter from Lagos usually arrives via email but it can turn up in the post, although this method is much rarer. It's far easier to lure a victim with the click of a mouse rather than hope for a letter or phone call back. It's also far safer from the scammer's point of view to hide contact details behind the veil of a computer connection.

Relative values

A variation on this theme is an email or letter saying that a couple and their only son have died in an air crash, leaving a small fortune with no one to inherit it. The money will pass to the relevant government unless it is claimed soon – so the pressure to act quickly is on. The message purports to come from a solicitor, or the equivalent in a foreign country, who acted for the deceased and has control of the estate.

Now it so happens that you have the same surname as the unlucky couple and the bogus solicitor suggests that you claim to be the nearest surviving relative. There is no pretence that this is anything other than fraud. The letter makes it clear that the solicitor is well aware that you are not really related, but you and he will split the proceeds and no one will ever find out.

Just to make it look authentic, you may be sent a copy of, or a link to, a news story about the crash. The crash is genuine, just not the inheritance.

It is quite possible that someone with your surname will be mentioned as being among the dead. It makes sense for the scammer to look through the phone book or the electoral role for people with the right surname so the scam will have a better chance of success.

One hopes that they are more careful than the scammer who sent me such a letter, giving his address as being just off the Old Kent Road. How stupid can you get? Apart from the fact that I live near enough to visit the address, you don't impress people by claiming to live on the cheapest road in the London Monopoly set.

Whose bank account is it anyway?

The whole purpose of obtaining your bank details is not to put money in – it is to take money out. You will find the entire contents removed double-quick time into an overseas bank account which will itself be emptied of cash and closed down. There is no way of tracking the perpetrators.

Another cunning aspect is that if the scam is blatantly fraudulent or illegal you will be reluctant to go to the authorities to complain, or to ask your bank to try to recover the money, as you will be implicating yourself as well as the scammers.

Letters from history

Like many modern scams, the Letter from Lagos has been around in one form or another for a lot longer than we think, so people must keep falling for it or it would die a natural death. It occurred more than a century ago as the Spanish Prisoner scam. The start of the letter from this episode is a little old-fashioned, but the general tone is rather familiar:

> "Although I know you only from good references of your honesty, my sad situation compels me to reveal to you an important affair in which you can procure a modest fortune, saving at the same time that of my darling daughter."

This type of letter probably started going out as soon as the Royal Mail was established in 1516 and certainly since the postal service as we know it began when postage stamps were invented in 1837.

An article in the *New York Times* in 1898 described the scam, much as we know it today, under the headline: 'An old swindle revived'. So it was considered old even then. The newspaper quoted police authorities as saying the swindle had been in operation for more than 30 years. The article read:

> "A man in this country receives a letter from a foreign city, written as fairly well-educated foreigners write English, with a word misspelled here and there, and an occasional foreign idiom. The writer is always in jail because of some political offense. He always has some large sum of money hid and is invariably anxious that it should be recovered. He knows of the prudence and good character of the recipient of the letter through a mutual friend, whom he does not mention for reasons of caution, and appeals to him in time of extremity for

help. He is willing to give one-third of the concealed fortune to the man who will recover it."

One such swindle reported in the article involved a letter supposedly written by Serge Solovieff, an imprisoned Russian banker who needed help recovering funds he had hidden in America. The envelope enclosed a newspaper clipping about Solovieff's arrest.

Various copies of this letter have subsequently emerged, suggesting that they were produced en masse, though the task was a little more painstaking in the days when missives had to be copied out by hand. They are written in different handwriting, so we can assume that none were actually from Solovieff.

The Russian banker may have been a real person who was actually arrested and imprisoned. If so, it would add credibility to the appeal for assistance, just as the scam in its modern form often contains links to genuine newspaper reports of people being killed or arrested. The basic principles have not changed in over 100 years.

The French connection

Another recorded example of the scam, showing how easily it crosses international boundaries, cropped up even earlier in the 19th century, this time in France.

An American translation of the Memoirs of Eugène François Vidocq, who described himself as a principal agent of the French police up to 1827, told how French prisoners obtained the addresses of rich people living in a wide area surrounding the prison and wrote what became known as letters of Jerusalem.

An example given in the book is from a prisoner claiming to have worked as a valet for a marquis. This is the translation:

"Sir,--You will doubtlessly be astonished at receiving a letter from a person unknown to you, who is about to ask a favour from you; but from the sad condition in which I am placed, I am lost if some honourable person will not lend me succour: that is the reason of my addressing you, of whom I have heard so much that I cannot for a moment hesitate to confide all my affairs to your kindness. I emigrated with my master, and that we might avoid suspicion we travelled on foot and I carried the luggage, consisting of a casket containing 16,000 francs in gold and the diamonds of the late marchioness."

In order to conceal their identities in transit, the writer says he and the marquis had to abandon and hide their gold-and-diamond filled casket. When the writer was sent back for the money, he was apprehended before retrieving it, and imprisoned for not having a passport.

In this case it was not the contents of a bank account that the scammer wanted, but he did want money – to buy his release from jail. The victim of the scam was to bribe the authorities to release the prisoner, whereupon the casket would be recovered and the benefactor immediately rewarded.

In reality the freed prisoner would have done a bunk at the earliest opportunity.

Vidocq reckoned that one person in five receiving the letter fell for it, which is a pretty high success rate.

How the Letter from Lagos scam has changed over the years

The beauty of this scam is that it can be adapted so easily to changes in social conditions while playing on the perennial attraction of get-rich-quick schemes. Every time there is media publicity about the scam, it lies dormant until enough people have forgotten about the dangers.

The Letter from Lagos has been given a new lease of life by the internet and social media, which have made communication with complete strangers across the globe quite commonplace.

The internet also means that scammers can communicate more quickly, widely and easily with a wider range of potential victims.

Television news makes us more aware of disasters in far-flung places that can be used to add an air of authenticity to hard luck stories.

Why do people fall for it?

It must be the hypnotic $ signs that cause the victims to suspend disbelief. Instinct tells us when an offer of riches is too good to be true, yet we go along with it just in case it turns out to be the offer of a lifetime.

Other false attractions based on erroneous assumptions are:

- The plan seems so simple that nothing can go wrong.

- If we have miscalculated and something DOES go wrong, then the other person is the one who gets into trouble.

- The scheme costs us nothing.

- We are helping to right a grievous wrong.

- We are helping someone living in poverty through no fault of their own to make a better life for themselves.

We would do better to ask ourselves the obvious questions, such as why on earth would a complete stranger thousands of miles away want to risk transferring money into our account? If, as they make out, they really are stuck in poverty in a remote African village, how come they have access to an internet connection and a bank account that allows them to transfer money abroad? What recourse do they have if we do the dirty on them and keep the money?

If millions of pounds are transferred out of one account into the account of a completely unrelated party in a different country, is it not likely to arouse suspicion within the banking system? Do you think the corrupt foreign government would fail to notice? How would it get past the strict foreign currency controls?

If the money is already in another country, say Switzerland, and the person who contacted you has access to it, why don't they go and collect it? After all, it will be no easier collecting the money from you.

These are the sorts of questions that you should ask yourself when you receive any approach that could be a scam.

How we can beat the scammers

The simple answer is to delete these emails immediately. Warn other people if you see a new twist to the scam.

If you want to get rich quickly, you stand a better chance in a national lottery. Although the odds are heavily stacked against you, at least some people win and you limit your losses to however many tickets you buy.

*   *   *

If you want to help impoverished people in the developing world, find a charity that offers genuine aid.

From a scam that is generally petty and pervasive, let us now move on to one that is big, brash and highly selective.

CHAPTER 4.
The Goebbels Scam

IT WAS JOSEPH GOEBBELS, THE NAZI PROPAGANDIST, WHO said that if you're going to tell a lie, tell a big one. He often followed his own advice. Sometimes people believe a real whopper because they don't think anyone would have the nerve to make it up.

You may feel that only the wealthy are targeted by really outrageous scams but this is not always so. It is true that rich people are preferred targets as they can be conned out of more money, but anyone can fall for this type of scam. Remember that scammers can be remarkably plausible.

After you have been taken in you may choose to suffer in silence because you feel so foolish to have fallen for a story that looks utterly ludicrous with the benefit of hindsight.

Perhaps more than any other scam, this is the one where your brain tells you not to be so stupid but your heart overrules it. It's the scam where you have a sneaking admiration for the perpetrator, where the stories can be quite funny – as long as you are not the victim.

The Eiffel Tower

Scams don't come much bigger than the 'sale' of the Eiffel Tower. The iron lattice edifice was built by engineer Gustave Eiffel as the entrance arch to the Exposition Universelle, a world's fair to celebrate the centennial of the French Revolution in 1889.

The design was panned by some leading artists and intellectuals but it has become one of the most recognisable structures in the world, the very symbol of Paris, and has been visited by approaching 300 million tourists, including Goebbels' boss Adolph Hitler. At 324 metres (1,063 ft) tall, it was at one time the tallest man-made structure in the world and is still the tallest building in Paris.

The tower still held this world record when, in March 1925, it was closed temporarily for routine renovations. Con artist Victor Lustig saw his chance. Granting himself the title of Count to sound more authentic and impressive, he called together the major scrap merchants in and around Paris and told them that the tower was to be demolished.

This was not as far fetched as it now sounds. The original intention, well publicised during the competition among designers for the structure to stand on the Champ de Mars, was for the tower to stand for 20 years and then it would be dismantled. The Eiffel Tower was already 16 years past its allotted time span but had been saved because the radio aerial on the top was so useful for communications.

The scrap merchants were told that they would easily cover the cost of demolition because they would keep the 7,300 tonnes of wrought iron. 'Count' Lustig told them to submit sealed bids to him and the highest bidder would take the contract.

Lustig seems to have been a good judge of character (which is more than can be said for the scrap merchants). He worked out which contractor looked the shadiest and told him privately that in return for a hefty bribe, Lustig would open ensure he came out narrowly on top in the bidding. The wheeze worked – Lustig cashed the cheque paid by the rogue contractor and caught the next train to Vienna.

Lustig is reputed to have got away with his Eiffel Tower scam twice, thanks to the reluctance of his victims to publicise their own stupidity and crooked behaviour.

The scam has a modern resonance. Where you are invited to take part in something that is supposedly lucrative but is clearly illegal, it is hard to complain to the police because you are admitting to your own guilt.

Monuments man

Another 1920s man who thought large was Arthur Ferguson, and although reports of his exploits may have been exaggerated he is known to have pulled off his own version of selling famous landmarks.

Ferguson realised that it is generally easier to fool a foreigner than a local. Ignorance can be exploited. So when he put Nelson's Column in Trafalgar Square up for sale he picked on an American tourist as his victim – a man who was not only lacking knowledge of the United Kingdom, but also someone with money. Poor Americans could not afford holidays in London.

Ferguson was also plausible. He said that the UK was selling Nelson's Column because it needed to clear national debts built up in the first world war.

To avoid arousing suspicion, he refrained from looking too desperate to clinch a deal, telling the American that the British government would sell only to someone who would appreciate the monument. A trick scammers like to play is to persuade their victim to beg to be defrauded.

The rich tourist paid £6,000, a princely sum in those days. Quite how he thought he could dismantle the column and take it away is not known.

Ferguson went on to raise £1,000 from the sale of the clock tower at the Houses of Parliament popularly known as Big Ben and accepted a downpayment of £2,000 on Buckingham Palace.

It is claimed that London became too hot for him and that he fled to the United States, where he leased out the White House for a year for $100,000, and was caught trying to sell the Statue of Liberty for a similar amount.

How the Goebbels scam has changed over the years

The drawback of this scam was that it could be used only on very rich people who could afford to buy into the outrageous dream.

However, the idea of telling a massive lie in the hope that it goes unchallenged can be adapted into virtually every scam there is.

How we can beat the scammers

- Be ready to challenge any story you are told, especially if it sounds improbable.

- Look at the details and think about where there is a catch.

- Don't accept the word of a complete stranger.

- Don't let the scammer play on your vanity.

- Above all else, if it sounds too good to be true, don't even think about it.

Goebbels scams typically involve few people and often depend on secrecy. In contrast, our next scam courts publicity and works on the basis of the more the merrier.

CHAPTER 5.
Pyramid Frauds

W HEN PYRAMIDS WERE BUILT IN EGYPT AND CENTRAL America, it seemed to be the most solid method of constructing huge structures that would last forever. Indeed, they are still there thousands of years later.

The structure gets wider from top to bottom, so the lower layers can fully support the upper ones. The centre of gravity goes straight down the middle, so it can't topple over.

Alas, the opposite happens with pyramid schemes, where one person at the top recruits another, wider layer of people, who recruit a wider layer of people below them, and so on. Common sense tells you that this cannot go on ad infinitum. The further you are down the layers, the heavier the burden that is crushing you from above. Only the people in the higher layers come out with the goodies.

The chain letter

Pyramid schemes can be perfectly legal. To see how they operate, and why they are basically flawed, let us consider the humble chain letter. This mode of communication resurfaces from time to time and, as so often with con tricks, it disappears until enough people have forgotten that they don't work and a new generation reaches the age of consent to be fleeced.

Details can vary but a typical scheme is one that taught me at the age of 11 that chain letters don't work. It was the first and last time I fell for such a scheme. It worked, or rather didn't work, like this:

You receive a letter with four names and addresses on it. You send a postcard of your own locality to the name at the top of the list, then remove the top name from the list and add your own name and address on to the bottom. You send on the new list to four people you know with instructions to do likewise.

The letter promised that, as my name gradually rose to the top, I would soon receive 256 postcards from various locations, some possibly from abroad. I dutifully sent off a postcard of the village where I lived to the name at the top of the list and passed the chain letter on to four friends. I received not a single postcard for my trouble.

A quick check of the mathematics tells you why chain letters cannot work. To reach me, the letter must have already been distributed to at least 256 people. If each of them passes the letter on to four people, that takes the total above 1,000. Another five layers takes us to 1 million; five layers after that we are up to 1 billion.

From the start of the letter, it has to be passed on only 17 times and there will not be enough people left in the entire world to form the next layer!

Chain mail can be accompanied by moral blackmail, threats or promises of riches. If it comes to you in email form it is possible that passing it on can alert fraudsters to the fact that your email address is active and that you are gullible. Ignoring chain mail is a good lesson in developing the mentality for not getting sucked into scams.

Multi-level marketing

Forming a pyramid can be a legitimate way of selling goods and services. It is known in the trade as multi-level marketing and it works like this:

The person at the top of the pyramid recruits agents to do the actual selling in return for a percentage of the sales. The agents in the second layer are free to recruit new agents, again in return for a percentage of the sales. Thus any agent at the third level is earning money for themselves and two people higher up the pyramid.

These agents are free to recruit another lower level of agents who will now find that much of the commission they earn is swallowed up by people above them.

Eventually, if too many layers are recruited, the pyramid reaches a point where the people at the bottom cannot possibly earn a living. At this level there is heavy turnover of agents as they become disillusioned. Inevitably, as with the chain letter, there are insufficient people to sell the products to.

The disadvantages of such a scheme are:

- Success depends on continuously getting new recruits and there is a limit to how many distributors can be found.

- There is a limit to how many products can be sold.

- Distributors may have been pressured into joining a scheme they are not really interested in and have no skills to turn it into a success.

- New agents often have to pay a large fee to join the scheme and buy products up front, so they find themselves out of pocket when they fail to meet sales targets.

We can see that even when a pyramid scheme is legal it is fraught with difficulties for the unwary. If it is a scam you will part with money up front and get nothing in return. Scammers can vanish with amazing speed.

This brings us to a frequent theme of this book, which is: if in doubt, walk away.

If you are tempted, here are some basic rules:

- Remember there is no easy way to wealth.

- Check whether there is a real product or service that consumers actually want and whether you can return unsold items for a full refund.

- Never sign up on the spot – go home and sleep on it. If the scheme is genuine it will still be there in the morning.

- If you are told to sign on the spot or miss the opportunity, then you must walk away. No organisation of bullies is worth getting involved with. Your weakness will be used against you to extort more money from you.

- Be prepared to take professional or legal advice.

The Give and Take scheme

Anyone can fall for a pyramid scam and they may be more prevalent than you realise. Nine women aged between 30 and 70 were found guilty of promoting a pyramid scheme in the first case of its kind in the UK brought under the Consumer Protection from Unfair Trading Act 2008.

Victims were encouraged to "beg, borrow or steal" to invest in the Give and Take scheme, as it was called, on the assurance that they "could not lose". An estimated £21 million was raised between May 2008 and April 2009, supposedly to be placed in high yielding investments as the economy recovered from the financial crash.

The lucky ones were those who invested early and got their money out before the scheme collapsed. Not so lucky were 88% of investors who lost between £3,000 and £15,000 as their cash was used to pay off the first wave of investors and put £92,000 into the pockets of each of the committee members behind the scheme.

The Ponzi scheme

The basic principles of the pyramid scheme, and evidence of why it is suspect, can be found in one of the most famous types of fraud: the Ponzi scheme.

It refers to an investment fund where the rewards on offer are so great that they cannot possibly be met from returns on any investments that the fund makes. Dividends for the original investors are paid out of new money pouring in. This type of scheme can work for several years, because the payment of dividends wins over the sceptics, who start to believe that the scheme is genuine after all.

Inevitably, though, like all pyramids that depend on ever increasing numbers of newcomers propping up the top of the structure, Ponzi schemes eventually collapse under their own weight.

The scheme is named after Charles Ponzi, who was born in Italy in 1882 but emigrated to the United States. His scheme was launched in 1920 and lasted little more than a year.

To be fair to poor old Ponzi, he probably didn't intend to set up the type of scheme that bears his name. It wasn't even his idea – apparently he got the notion from his bookmaker, who claimed to have made $1 million from doing something similar.

It all sounds ludicrous nearly 100 years later, but Ponzi proposed to acquire postal coupons from contacts in Italy and sell them to fellow Italian immigrants for use in sending letters and parcels back to the old country. It was perfectly legal and it slashed the cost of postage between the US and Italy. Ponzi promised to return 50% profit in 45 days or 100% in 90 days, theoretically possible if the scheme worked. He took in $20 million in a little over 12 months.

Naturally the US postal service was alarmed. It would be handling post at the American end but the Italian postal service would collect the revenue. It had turned a blind eye to this loophole when it was exploited on a small scale but it could not tolerate an organised operation running on an industrial scale.

The arrangement seemed to be legal, so the American postal service did the one thing it could: prevaricate until the problem went away. It refused to accept the Italian coupons while it decided whether to continue to accept them. All it had to do was postpone a decision until Ponzi went bust.

The unfortunate Italian clung on while he could use money from new investors to keep the existing investors happy, but eventually a combination of factors – adverse press reports, a run of withdrawals and the attention of the Massachusetts banking commissioner – brought the scheme crashing down.

Ponzi served various terms in prison until he was released in 1934. He died in 1949 but, to rewrite a line from the famous Elton John song, his candle burnt out long before his legend ever will. The scheme that bears his name keeps recurring.

Ponzi reborn

Ponzi schemes crop up from time to time as people with more money than sense forget that if a scheme sounds too good to be true it should be treated with extreme caution. This brings us to the largest fraud perpetrated in US history.

Bernard Madoff was a stockbroker, investment adviser and financier, so he knew all about making money and handling other people's cash. Like Charles Ponzi, he probably did not set out to establish and run a Ponzi scheme.

He began collecting, investing and living well off other people's money in the 1990s and he was sufficiently successful to keep the ship afloat until the scandal broke in 2008. By the time it all unravelled, he had over the years collected $65 billion, of which $18 billion was missing.

Many clients were billionaires or celebrities such as Nicola Horlick and Steven Spielberg. But he also sucked in smaller investors, banks and charities, according to the *Wall Street Journal*.

One reason for Madoff's success was that he was a highly respected and well-established financial expert. He actually helped to found the NASDAQ stock exchange in New York and served a term as its chairman. NASDAQ specialises in hi-tech, high growth stocks and it has become the second largest stock exchange in the world.

He earned his investors' trust because whenever they requested a withdrawal he paid promptly. Unusually for a Ponzi scheme, he did not tempt investors by promising unrealistically high returns. What was suspicious was that the returns were remarkably consistent year on year, whereas genuine investments of all types have good and bad years.

This anomaly was not, however, enough to arouse the suspicions of the Securities and Exchange Commission (SEC), the United States financial watchdog. It was Madoff himself who eventually 'fessed up in December 2008. It seems that the strain of maintaining what he admitted was "just one big lie" became too much. Three months later he pleaded guilty to all charges of fraud against him and was sentenced to 150 years in prison.

And reborn again

Investors had barely recovered from the shock surrounding Madoff when another Ponzi scheme led by Texas billionaire banker Allen Stanford hit the headlines. Had Madoff not set the bar so high, Stanford's scheme would have been the biggest Ponzi fraud to date.

He managed to accumulate $8 billion over a decade from the sale of fraudulent certificates of deposit in his bank in Antigua. Unlike Madoff, Stanford attracted investors through interest rates that were too good to be true. Also unlike Madoff, some of Stanford's bank officials were in on the fraud.

In the wake of these two schemes, the SEC has stepped up investment regulation and fraud detection measures, but it will always be running a fire-fighting operation because these schemes often start off as legitimate investment operations and it is impossible to say at what point they will tip over into insolvency.

How the pyramid scam has changed over the years

This type of scam has probably changed least of all through time, certainly as far as the basics are concerned. In particular this type of scam offers potential rewards well above the average return on investments and it usually builds momentum in the early stages by meeting the promised returns, which lures in more punters.

With the greater financial regulation that is now in place perpetrators are more conscious of maintaining an image of respectability and financial probity.

How to beat the scammers

Ponzi schemes can be hard to spot because they appear on the surface to be legitimate. However, if you know what to look for and you're careful, you should be able to avoid them. Here's a checklist:

- **Fools rush in**: Never rush into an investment. The more you feel pressurised, the more you should resist.

- **Too good to be true**: When you're approached with an opportunity that seems unbelievably amazing, you should be highly suspicious. By all means do your research as far as you can, but be prepared to miss out rather than take a risk. If you find it difficult to get detailed information, assume that someone is trying to hide the facts from you.

- **Limit your loss:** Don't put all your cash into a risky investment. Never invest more than you can afford to lose.

- **Be cautious, even when an investment looks sound**: Ponzi schemes can last for some time and look to be built on firm foundations. Is the investment you are being offered regulated? Does it publish annual statements? Is it part of a compensation scheme if things go wrong?

As with the pyramid scheme, many scams inevitably involve the victim providing cash up front in the hope of greater rewards later. In the next chapter, we consider this in its basic form.

CHAPTER 6.
The Advance Fee Scam

THIS SCAM EXISTS IN MANY FORMS, BUT THE BASIC PRINCIPLE is this:

- You pay up front.
- You don't receive what you expected.
- There are then further fees to pay.
- You face the dilemma of whether to cut your losses or throw good money after bad.

Like many traditional scams, the advance fee scam has gained a new lease of life in the technological age because it is possible to target so many people quickly and easily.

Typical lures are:

- Lottery prizes
- Sales in investments

- Money transfers from abroad
- Compensation claims

The Letter from Lagos scam can operate as an advance fee fraud. You may be asked to make an upfront payment as a gesture of good faith so that the person supposedly transferring money into your account knows he can trust you.

Naturally you are led to believe that a small payout now will bring far greater rewards. And it is so easy. The fee covers all the paperwork, legal hurdles, etc., that the kind person on the other end of the phone will carry out for you. That's what the upfront fee is for.

There will often be key details missing from the information you are given so you cannot make inquiries to see if the supposed reward is genuine. Many of these fraudulent schemes have a foreign connection, which makes it harder for you to keep tabs on, or process, the claim yourself.

The obstacles pile up

It's all going through so smoothly when, alas, some unexpected obstacle crops up. There is an administrative fee that has to be paid. It's purely routine. Don't worry, everything is fine.

You have to pay banking charges, possibly in more than one country. Then there is a fee for actually transferring the funds. There will be bribes to pay to speed up the necessary authorisations. Failure to grease the palms of foreign officials means that the process grinds to a halt.

Each payment demanded may be quite small, certainly in comparison with the small fortune awaiting you, but the outlay can run to thousands of pounds, depending on the size of the potential gain. As each demand comes through, you are faced with the awful choice of writing off everything you have already spent or putting up more and more money. The scammer will continue with his demands until he has bled you dry or you finally face up to reality.

Scammers will prefer to get as much as they think you will pay upfront so it is harder for you subsequently to bite the bullet and drop out. If you do decide to face reality, they will already have taken you for a tidy sum.

We shall see another example of this scam in the next chapter when we look at the lottery scam. Other cases include the building work scam in Chapter 8.

Advance fees can be legitimate

Paying a fee upfront can be perfectly legitimate. If you book a hotel room you would not be surprised to be asked for a deposit. If you order goods online you pay when you order.

Sometimes an advance fee sits on the borderline between legitimacy and sharp practice. For instance, companies have bombarded people by telephone with offers to claim compensation for injury or banking malpractices. Often you can make the claims easily yourself without letting a third party take a hefty fee out of your entitlement, but if you choose to let them apply on your behalf you expect to pay for the service.

Similarly there is a dubious trade in applying for documents such as visas where you log onto a website dressed up to look like the official site. It's perfectly legal but you unsuspectingly pay an extra fee. Since you are filling in all the details yourself, you may as well do it on the official site at less cost.

How we can beat the scammers

The only answer to the advance fee scam is not to be sucked into it in the first place:

- If you are supposed to have won a prize, tell them to take their cut out of the winnings.

- Buy goods, assets and services from people you choose to approach, not from complete strangers who approach you.

- Do not even think about paying up front to get involved in any project that is blatantly illegal.

- Asking for cash up front is very popular with scammers, partly because they can't lose and partly because it can be adapted to different situations, as we shall see in the next chapter.

CHAPTER 7.

The Lottery Scam

M**ANY OF US LIKE A FLUTTER. WE ALSO LIKE THE IDEA OF** getting something for nothing, or very nearly nothing, so the prospect of winning anything from a cuddly toy to millions of pounds in return for a ticket costing £1 or less proves hard to resist. This is what makes lotteries so attractive.

A lottery has three essential ingredients:

1. You have to pay to enter the game.

2. There is at least one prize.

3. Prizes are awarded purely on chance.

No doubt lotteries go back in some form or another to time immemorial. The first recorded existence in the UK was in 1569, when the organisers of a state lottery sold tickets at the west door of St. Paul's Cathedral in London.

Of course, lotteries are often entirely legal. National lotteries exist in many countries with government blessing, raising money for good causes and other developments. At the other end of the scale, local charities can buy a lottery licence to fund worthwhile pet projects.

Gambling regulation

Whatever the reason – fundraising or just fun – lotteries are a form of gambling and are covered by the Gambling Act 2005. Except for the National Lottery, regulation is the responsibility of the Gambling Commission.

While there is no maximum price for a ticket, in each lottery all tickets must cost the same. That way, everyone has the same chance of winning for the same outlay.

So by all means buy a lottery ticket for a bit of fun and to support a cause dear to your heart. If you win, it's icing on the cake.

There is no limit on the size of the prize, which can be in cash, goods or services. However, as an investment, buying lottery tickets is a pretty lousy choice, even when legal. Half the price of your ticket tends to go in running costs plus donations to good causes. Never think of a lottery as something for nothing. You and others like you are paying in some form or another.

And yet, some people apparently think that they can win a lottery without even buying a ticket. So when they are told by letter, email or telephone call that they have won a prize they think it is their lucky day.

It does not occur to them that someone must pay for this prize and the logical conclusion is that they and other victims will end up paying more than the value of the prize – even if a prize exists, which is not always the case.

You're a Euromug

A friend was visiting my house when she received a mobile phone call from her sister, who proclaimed excitedly that she had won a large sum of money on the EuroMillions. Nothing could persuade the sister that, as she had not bought a ticket for the current lottery, she could not possibly have won. She had bought tickets in the past so it must have been an old ticket that had come up trumps.

She had received the news by phone. The caller had reassured her by saying that to prove it was genuine he would give her a number she could ring back on. This was no guarantee at all, as scammers can easily rent telephone lines for a short time and then disappear. Many fraudulent telephone calls come from overseas anyway and are beyond the reach of national regulators.

She was also given a fax number to send over her bank details for the money to be deposited. Are alarm bells ringing? Not with the lady in question, though they should have been. People who ask for your bank details can be quite adept at removing money from your account rather than putting it in.

The call was indeed a scam and the only saving grace was that the woman in question had very little in her account, so when it was raided she got off lightly.

The first shall be least

Sometimes you will receive a letter or telephone call stating you have supposedly won one of a range of prizes, from a watch or piece of jewellery, up to a sum of money large enough to transform your life. You are GUARANTEED (always in capital letters) to have won something.

These prizes, at least the cheaper ones and possibly even more expensive ones, may actually exist but you can't find out what you have won until you have stumped up money in some form or another. Many prizes are cheap rubbish that someone wants to dump for whatever price they can get.

A particular favourite device is to force you to ring a premium rate telephone number to register your personal details. These calls tend to last at least three minutes and your personal details can be sold on to junk mail outfits that bombard you with fliers and possibly more scams. Remember, if you fall for one trick you are marked down as someone who is easily conned.

You may have to ring the premium rate number more than once, with calls lasting several minutes, which racks up more cash for the person you are calling.

It is not always obvious that you are ringing a premium rate, or even that you are paying for the call. If you get a pre-recorded phone call saying you have won a prize (for example a 'free' cruise) and all you have to do is press a button to claim, it all seems quite harmless. The caller is paying for the call, surely?

Not once you press the button, they aren't. You are now paying for the call at a premium rate.

It's your lucky day!

Another guise of this scam is where an official sounding organisation purportedly writes to inform you that you have won a very large prize in a foreign lottery. The sheer amount of the alleged winnings seems to blind people to the fact that they haven't entered the lottery and therefore can't possibly have won. You may not even have visited the country where the lottery is supposedly based.

The organisation contacting you claims to have the sole rights to inform winners of their good fortune and to claim the prize on their behalf. All you have to do is pay a fee to cover expenses and the prize will be claimed for you.

Ask yourself these questions:

- Did I buy this lottery ticket?
- Why were you not informed of the win by the lottery company itself?
- How can a third party have the right to be informed of winners' names and addresses?
- Why can't the third party take its expenses out of the winnings?

The only possible answer is that neither the ticket nor the prize exist, and quite probably the lottery company doesn't either.

Lottery scams are often dressed up with the name of a well-known and respected organisation to make them look legitimate. I received the following missive, which rather amusingly refers to "those that has been scammed":

United Nations Compensation Award 2014
Approved Your Payment

United Nations Assisted Program

Directorate Of International Payment And Transfers.

Transfer/Audit Unit

Our Ref: WB/NF/JPP/UN/XX-321/02014

Attention : Sir/Madam . I would like to let it be known that in a meeting held by the United Nations in Affiliation with the World Bank Organization and the U.S States Government, it has been agreed that a compensation of

USD$6.5 Million has been approved in your name. This Compensation program was organized to compensate all the people who have in time past had unfinished transaction and those that has been scammed in any part of the world. This compensation scheme was set up under the United Nations Project for unsettled debts and scam victims rehabilitation scheme.

Your E-mail Address was drawn automatically web directory through an E-mail ballot machine, that is why this mail was sent to you and you are qualified to receive the above mentioned compensation payment.

A Bank Draft Ref No: 4083 0521 431 00114 has been allocated to you which will be credited with your payment of US$6.5 Million Dollars which will be delivered to you in person at your place of residence.

You are hereby advised to contact Bank Manager of Zenith Bank Plc in the name of Dr.Jim Ovia at the address below for your payment :

Contact Person : Dr.Jim Ovia.

Bank Name : Zenith Bank Plc

Email: zenithbank-ng-plc@cd2.com

Personal Phone: +234814-773-2008

You are also instructed to forward the following information below to the above Bank for complete processing and delivery of your Bank Draft to you.

1. Your Full Name :

2. Your Home/Mobile Telephone No:

3. Your Home or Office Address :

4. Age/Occupation/Marital Status:

5. Country OF ORIGIN:

You are advised to contact the Zenith at the address above, and have your information listed above forwarded to them with 72 hrs you receive this message to avoid cancelation of your payment.

Thanks for your patience, and do contact us in the near future when you have successfully received your payment.

Best Regard, Ms. Valerie Amos.

One hopes that the United Nations employs better speakers of English on its staff. It would take an awful lot of scams for me to part with the equivalent of $6.5 million, even if I had that sort of money in the first place.

If you were to get a message like this, you'd have to ask yourself:

- Why is the United Nations compensating people for scams?

- Why is it sending out badly written messages?

- Why is it apparently drawing people's names out of a hat to decide who gets compensation?

- Why is it using a Nigerian bank? (A quick check on the internet provided details of Zenith Bank, which does legitimately exist.)

- Why does it address the message to "Dear Sir or Madam"?

- Why does it need all those personal details when all the bank draft needs is my name, which the sender supposedly already has?

- Why issue a bank draft anyway rather than process a payment directly into my bank account?

Scoring an own goal

Another fake win with an international flavour was this one:

Esa Seppälä (esa.seppala@educ.goteburg.se)

You are one of the six lucky Winner of One Million Pounds in Abu Dhabi Manchester City promotion 2014. Contact Agrent Mrs Esa Lars Kuja. via E-mail: info@manchester. hyperoffice.com Contact with your Serial number ABY-433-9966-6679. For more information.

Best Regards,

Online Co-ordinate

Mrs Esa Lars Kuja.

So let's get this straight. An English football club (which I don't happen to support) is running a lottery in Abu Dhabi (which I have never visited), and the winners are being notified by an education establishment in Sweden (where I've never been educated).

Something doesn't quite add up. Oh, and I hadn't bought a ticket in the first place.

The email address book at the education establishment in Gothenburg had probably been hacked. The same could be said of one in the Middle East, which was used to send out this ambitious offering:

Shamekh m. ElShamy (smshamy@uqu.edu.sa)

Your email ID has been give the sum of 3,000,000.00 pounds in the ongoing jumbo end of year draw. For claims send your

Full names

Address

Tel

Country to email : jumblott111@outlook.com

These inappropriate email addresses are often a clue to the dubious nature of the message for those who have difficulty in grasping the blindingly obvious. And one may wonder why Coca-Cola Europe sends out winning notifications from the ambulance service in Victoria, Australia, as below.

Hoffman, Peter (peter.hoffman@ambulance.vic. gov.au)

From: Hoffman, Peter (peter.hoffman@ambulance.vic. gov.au)

Win $750,000 in Coca Cola Company Europe yearly promo. To qualify, Email the correct answer to the question given below to Mr. Frank Joe via email (mrfrankjoe_desk12@torba.com) Question: Who won the 2010 FIFA World Cup in South Africa? (A) Usa (B) Spain (C) Australia (China)

This scammer has at least grasped the basic point that people need to enter a competition to win it. Don't be tempted to try your luck. If there really is such a competition it will be on the company's website. Visit the site directly to enter the competition there.

Passage to India

One of the most heart-rending stories arising from a lottery scam concerned a man living in a remote village in India. The only consolation was that the scammers did not make him part with any money – but only because he didn't have any.

Ratan Kumar Malbisoi was a 41-year-old unemployed man with little formal education living in Orissa state. He fell for a message on his mobile phone saying he had won the BBC's National Lottery and his prize was worth more than £200,000. Although the BBC does not run a lottery itself, it does broadcast the draw for the British National Lottery.

Mr Malbisoi was asked to send personal details to the scammers and he actually spoke to them several times over two years, begging them to send the promised funds to his bank account, for which he provided details.

No doubt the scammers refused to believe that a man who owned a mobile phone and had a bank account could possibly be poverty stricken so they kept playing him along. Eventually he borrowed money from some friends and walked 1,000 miles to the BBC office in New Delhi. He arrived during a cold spell wearing only a shirt and a pair of trousers and spent the night on a railway platform.

Mr Malbisoi told a BBC reporter that one of the scammers, who claimed to be 'BBC Chancellor', was well spoken and asked for payment of just over £100 to cover the cost of transferring the winnings to India. Over the two years this was negotiated down to the equivalent of about £40 but, with even this sum beyond his means, Mr Malbisoi decided to walk to New Delhi and claim the money over the counter. He took some convincing that it was a scam.

How we can beat the scammers

There are steps you can take to protect yourself from this nonsense:

- You have to be in it to win it, so if you didn't buy a ticket you haven't won.

- Always look for a catch – there are often very obvious loopholes in the story if you stop to think.

- Never pay upfront to collect your winnings.

- Never give your bank account or card details to callers.

While scammers often prefer to keep a distance between themselves and their victims, so it is easier to remain anonymous and make a quick getaway if necessary, we will see in the next chapter that they may choose to be up close and personal.

CHAPTER 8.
In Your Face Scams

W E NO LONGER HAVE DICK TURPIN SITTING ASTRIDE Black Bess at the top of Highgate Hill waiting to relieve stagecoach passengers of their purses, but it is remarkable how willing people are to hand over their cash or possessions to a trustworthy-looking person who approaches them.

From the fraudster's point of view, this type of scam works best when the situation can be manipulated such that the victim is begging to be fleeced and the scammer appears reluctant to take advantage.

My favourite story is a relatively harmless version that I witnessed living in Hong Kong in the late 1970s. A young man stood outside the driving test centre selling lucky charms for HK$5 each, which was less than 50p at the time. They probably cost HK$1 each to make.

Who could resist such a small outlay, because the charms came with a guarantee that you would pass your driving test, confidently backed by a promise of a money-back guarantee if you failed. That promise was always kept to those who produced their fail slips. Of course it was. The returned charms could be sold to another sucker later. Those who passed would not ask for a refund as they thought the charm had worked. The seller could not lose.

This con was so simple and it had a characteristic rare in the world of tricksters: it relied on a low profit per transaction but high turnover.

Watch and wait

A scam where people willingly handed over the loot to a man who looked trustworthy formed possibly the first scam to be reported in the press, back in 1849. The report concerned William Thompson, who was known as 'the confidence man'. Thompson would chat to strangers until he asked if they had the confidence to lend him their watches.

Amazingly, according to the report of Thompson's trial, several did just that, whereupon he would walk off with the watch. Thompson was captured when one of his victim's later recognised him on the street.

Robbed at the Ritz

A watch featured in another, even more daring, scam where the victim was persuaded to hand over the booty in a carefully engineered transatlantic fraud. This modern-day story demonstrates that even highly intelligent, sophisticated and successful businessmen can be outwitted by credible fraudsters.

John Hunter Maxwell, a former banker who had also been director-general of the Automobile Association, bought a rare watch made by legendary Swiss manufacturer Patek Philippe as an investment. This was quite a timepiece. Among other attributes it had a perpetual calendar, phases of the moon and it adjusted automatically for leap years. Presumably it also told the time.

Three years later, Mr Maxwell decided to cash in his investment. It was a snip at his asking price of £380,000. Another one was subsequently sold at auction for £15.6 million.

Maxwell arranged to sell his watch through a London broker, who had been recommended by a friend and who was not a party to the scam. In May 2013, after an exchange of emails with a man posing as a buyer, Maxwell agreed to hand the watch over once the agreed sale price had been deposited in his bank account.

The supposed purchaser insisted on making payment into an offshore bank account, which perhaps should have aroused suspicions, but as Maxwell had an account in Monaco that was not a problem.

Taking the Michael

What followed was simple yet highly organised. The fraudsters stole the identity of a member of the bank staff in Monaco and made a phone call and sent emails in the staff member's name to confirm that the money had been deposited. In fact, no money had been put into Maxwell's account.

At this stage Maxwell was in New York but he instructed his London agent to hand over the watch in good faith. The agent met a man called Michael at the Ritz Hotel in Piccadilly, London, and gave him the prized possession.

CCTV footage viewed later showed 'Michael' leaving the Ritz pretty sharpish and hurrying down the pavement and across the road. It is believed that the watch left the country with equal haste.

Be suspicious of dealing with people you have never met, especially those who want to deal through unusual channels. It can be better to sell an expensive item through a recognised auction house or saleroom, even if it means paying a hefty commission.

Doorstep scams

It's funny how often workmen just happen to be in your street. They've been doing work at another house just down the road or round the corner. The address is one you are likely to know but is just far enough away to mean that you don't know the occupants and are unlikely to check whether they really have had work done.

The product or service may actually be genuine. It is possible that these people really do have a load of bitumen left over that can be used on your drive, or perhaps they really do trim trees and have spotted a suspect branch on the one in your front garden.

Cold callers at your front door, however, should be treated with the same caution as cold callers on the telephone.

Consider the work that supposedly involves using something left over from another job:

- Are you accepting goods that someone else has paid for and is therefore entitled to?

- Have the goods been stolen rather than left over?

- What quality are the goods? Are they fit for purpose?

- How much are you actually paying for goods that will seemingly otherwise go to waste?

- Are you paying an excessive price for the labour involved, thus losing the benefits of getting cut-price goods?

An offer to do a job that you didn't know you needed doing (and you almost certainly don't need doing) is more common because it tends to be more lucrative for the scammer:

- He has the moral high ground because he claims he is doing you a favour.

- You can be persuaded that disaster is lurking if the job is left undone – for example rain will get into the rafters if roof tiles are not replaced.

- Since all goods and equipment are being supplied by the caller, you have no way of checking whether you really are getting anything on the cheap, so the price can be ramped up accordingly.

- More 'problems' can be discovered once the work has started, adding to the bill.

- They can rely on victims being unable to supervise the work as it will be a skilled job, possibly in an inaccessible place such as the roof.

Whatever the job, the perpetrators will make sure they get paid. If in doubt, they will demand money up front in the form of cash or card payment. They will not take cheques because they can easily be cancelled.

They are quite prepared to march the weak and vulnerable down to a cash point and force the victim to draw out cash, using more than one card if necessary. Better still, victims can be taken to their nearest bank branch where there will be no limit on the withdrawal.

The victim will find it is impossible to trace the perpetrators when it turns out that the work has been done shoddily or not at all. There will be no warranty guaranteeing the work for a set number of years, and no aftercare service. You may not even have their phone number.

You may feel tempted to have the work done because paying in cash means that you evade VAT. Remember that if you act illegally you will be in no position to complain to the authorities about unsatisfactory work. You won't be getting a proper receipt with the company's name and registered address on it so you will have no proof that you paid anybody anything.

Ask for identification

It helps if you ask for identification and write down the name, address and telephone number of anyone calling at your door. Get a business card if you can. Genuine door-to-door salespersons, like meter readers and council officials, will have badges dangling from their necks.

This is not a guarantee that the caller is genuine, since fake badges can easily be printed from any computer, but on the other hand if the caller refuses to give any identification of himself or the company he works for you know there is something dodgy about him.

The more pressure the caller puts on you, the harder it is to say no, but the more important it is that you do so. If the work really does need doing, you want to be all the more certain that it is done properly by a reliable company with the right tools, materials and experience.

There is only one way to find out if the quote you are being given is fair and that is to ask for other companies, ones that you know to be reputable, to quote for the work. Get prices, terms and warranty coverage down in writing, together with a written estimate of how long the work will take.

One vital word of warning when a stranger knocks on your door: put the chain on before you open it. That way it is much easier to say no and close the door. Never feel guilty about doing so. These people prey on the weak and the vulnerable and have no conscience about taking a victim's life savings.

Let him walk off in a huff. Don't let these people make you feel guilty. It's your home, not theirs.

Government projects

Unfortunately, cold-call scammers touting property improvements can be helped unintentionally by government initiatives. There's nothing like a do-good project where the government splashes taxpayers' money around to gladden the heart of a fraudster.

Any scam that can be linked to a well-publicised but only vaguely understood project is fertile ground for luring in the unwary. Cold callers try, if possible, to give the impression that they actually work for government and have official sanction. Bait to persuade you to let them loose on your house includes:

- This is your entitlement.

- You are getting this service at a highly subsidised rate.

- You will recover the small charge in a very short time because of the savings the work will generate.

- You are getting something that is very much in your interests and will bring enormous benefits.

- You pay your taxes to government and the local council and now you are getting something back. It's only fair. Look at what the benefit scroungers get.

- This offer has a limited time span so unless you act now you will miss out.

A great opportunity of this kind was created by the government initiative on energy savings in homes. With fuel and energy prices soaring and newspapers reporting looming energy shortages as out-of-date power stations are closed down without being replaced there is plenty of scope for spreading panic. Every personal crisis is an opportunity for those with initiative.

Double trouble

A report in the *Daily Telegraph* highlighted the case of a reader who had been approached by a salesman who told him of a government-backed scheme to install cavity wall insulation that would save the householder money and stop any issues with damp.

As the work was supported by a 25-year guarantee it seemed like a good idea. Less than a year later, the householder received a doorstep cold call from another salesman at a different company. He said that the installer who had insulated the property and others in the area had not done the job properly.

This salesman claimed that his wall insulating company worked in conjunction with a firm of solicitors and that they would redo the work, extracting the insulation and putting right any damage. They would sue the original installer and, since the whole scheme was government backed, they would recover the cost even if the original installer went bust.

The problem, according to the second salesman, was that the house had no damp-proof course, the brickwork had been damaged by frost, the pointing was of poor quality and there was sand up to one metre high in the cavities. He claimed that all this meant the house should never have had cavity wall insulation installed in the first place.

So which of the two installers was the cowboy and which the genuine article? Or were they both cowboys? It's impossible to say, which is why you should be wary of all cold callers.

The story turned out to have more twists than a detective novel when the *Telegraph* took up the case. The second salesman had produced a document called a deed of assignment which clearly stated on every page that his cavity insulation company was part of a group of solicitors.

The local office admitted that the insulation company was a client but failed to get back to the newspaper as promised. The head office of the solicitors said it strongly denigrated cold calling and would never knowingly accept instructions arising from a cold call. The cavity insulation company told the *Telegraph* that it never solicits work by knocking on doors. So perhaps the salesman did not actually work for it in the first place.

Are you confused by all that? Confusion is a very useful tool for scammers. If you don't understand, walk away.

The liar, the titch and the wardrobe

Empty houses have a special fascination for burglars. Some like the direct method of smashing their way in. Scammers prefer the thrill of a more subtle approach.

Followers of Sherlock Holmes will understand the literary allusion of the *Adventure of the Empty House* and there may indeed be a bit of detective work going on when a stranger knocks at your door. He may actually be hoping that no one answers because he is looking for an empty house.

The caller may be carrying a box of groceries to look as if he is a genuine delivery service. If you don't answer the door, he tries to burgle your house, but if you do answer he says he has a delivery for, say, Mrs Brown. You tell him that he has the wrong address and he wanders off to try his luck elsewhere. (If you happen to be called Brown there is no harm done because you will naturally deny having placed the order.)

A more sophisticated version of the empty house scam involves three people, a wardrobe and a large van. Two of the scammers find an empty house then knock on neighbours' doors trying to find someone with a key.

They produce paperwork showing that they are delivering a wardrobe that has been ordered, so you innocently let them in, wondering why your neighbour didn't let you know. Just to be on the safe side, you go in with the delivery men and the piece of furniture to make sure they don't steal anything, then you watch them drive away.

A little while later the men return. They have made a mistake and have delivered the wardrobe to the wrong address. Right number, wrong road. So you let them in and they remove the wardrobe, again under your supervision.

If you are particularly observant you might just notice that the wardrobe is a bit heavier for the men to carry out than it was going in. That is because a very light person, possibly a child, was inside the wardrobe all along and has filled it with cash, jewellery and anything else that is not too heavy and will fit in the available space.

The flatpack gang

One gang of four thought rather bigger than that. They planned to steal more than £1.5 million in gold bullion and jewellery from Rockefeller's, a showroom displaying jewellery and watches in Manchester.

The men first contacted the retailer by telephone posing as wealthy Italians and followed up with a visit by two of them who gave false names. Both were well dressed and wore Rolex watches. They ordered 41 highly valuable items including gold bullion and jewellery. Arrangements were made for a meeting at a hotel, where a Swiss banker would bring the cash to pay.

The gang booked into the hotel and assembled a flat pack cabinet. One of them hid inside. The idea was that the jeweller would be shown a case containing genuine cash, which would then be placed on the floor near the cabinet. While the sale was being agreed, the gang member in the cabinet would quietly switch the case for one containing counterfeit money.

On this occasion the police received a tip-off and they caught the gang red-handed. The four scammers, who had tried to pull similar stunts in London and Brighton, were all jailed. As the longest sentence was two years and eight months, it is easy to see why scammers are prepared to take the risk of getting caught.

How we can beat the scammers

Some lessons to be learnt are:

- Beware of cold callers. It is virtually impossible to tell the genuine companies from the cowboys. Do not allow strangers into your home.

- Ask for identification and make a note of details of any badge the caller shows. If there is a number on the badge, ring it to ask for confirmation that the caller is genuine, or even better use Google to search for the company on the internet. Even then you should remain suspicious.

- Look for holes in the stories. For example, how could a salesman possibly know there is sand blocking the cavity of your property without taking bricks out and looking inside?

- If you get contradictory information, believe nothing.

- You don't have to sign for anything straightaway. The greater the pressure on you to do so, the more likely it is to be a scam.

- Do not get sucked into litigation. Whatever promises are made to you about the certainty of winning, the outcome of court cases is always uncertain.

- Suing a rogue trader is particularly difficult as he is likely to disappear, leaving no assets behind.

- If you hold a key for a neighbour's house, make sure you have a phone number you can contact to check that someone asking to get into the property is legitimate.

In the next chapter we look at an even more pervasive scam that has affected most of us at some point.

CHAPTER 9.
Insurance Scams

THE ASSOCIATION OF BRITISH INSURERS (ABI) BELIEVES that 350 fraudulent insurance claims are made in the UK every single day – and those are just the ones where the perpetrators are caught. These daily claims totalled on average a staggering £3.6 million, or more than £1 Billion a year, which is twice the amount lost in shoplifting.

The ABI reckons that is only the tip of the iceberg. It estimates that there is a further £2 Billion annually of undetected fraud, all of which is adding an extra £50 to the annual household insurance bill.

Popular scams are:

- Slip and trip claims, where fraudsters falsely claim to have suffered injury in a fall.

- Dishonest motor insurance claims that totalled 67,000 cases worth £835 million – and that's only the total that was thwarted.

- Liability frauds, ranging from household and travel insurance to employer and public liability claims.

Three factors in particular have sent insurance claims soaring:

1. The idea has grown that cheating on an insurance claim is a victimless crime. It isn't. The victims are the honest members of the public who have to pay higher insurance premiums to cover the false claims.

2. The growth of claims management companies that bombard drivers and householders with cold calls and text messages.

3. The creation of 'no win, no fee' companies that make suing cheaper and less risky for complainants and more expensive and riskier for defendants.

Slip and trip scams

A 36-year-old man claimed £10,000 from supermarket chain Lidl, saying he had banged his head and hurt his side after slipping on a wet bag. CCTV from the Bradford store showed him lining up his foot with the bag and carefully lowering himself to the ground before calling for help.

He was later convicted of fraud by misrepresentation and given a ten-month suspended prison sentence.

A 30-year-old made a £17,000 claim against Newcastle City Council for the negligent maintenance of a drain which he allegedly fell over, breaking his ankle.

A YouTube video showed that he actually sustained the injuries while carrying out a stunt in front of a crowd in the city. The injuries prevented him from working so he filed a fraudulent claim. He later admitted fraud and was sentenced to 200 hours of community work and fined £600.

Fighting back

The insurance industry and the police are fighting back. The Insurance Fraud Bureau (IFB) was set up in 2006 as a not-for-profit company to lead the insurance industry's collective fight against insurance fraud. It acts as a central hub for sharing insurance fraud data and intelligence to detect and disrupt organised fraud networks. At any one time, 30 to 40 criminal gangs are under investigation by the IFB.

There is now also a dedicated police unit – the Insurance Fraud Enforcement Department. By cross-checking 130 million insurance policies and claims, the bureau identifies suspicious patterns of activity and tell-tale signs of organised fraud.

The crash for cash scam

You are driving along the road minding your own business when some lunatic shoots out from a side road right in front of you and slams on the brakes. To add insult to injury, the other driver blames you for the crash. You are a victim of the crash for cash scam.

It is estimated that about £400 million is claimed fraudulently every year in cash for crash scams. Possibly one-in-seven motoring claims is fraudulent, totalling the best part of 70,000 claims a year. In addition, insurers invest about £200 million a year in countering fraud.

Worse still, innocent people are at risk of injury or even death in the staged crashes. Their lives are disrupted. And the criminal gangs behind the fraud use the cash to fund other crimes such as illegal firearms, drug dealing and people trafficking.

The blame game

The aim is to stage accidents in which the innocent motorist looks to be to blame. In most collisions where a vehicle is shunted from the rear, the driver of the car behind is usually deemed to be at fault. There is an onus on drivers to stay far enough behind the vehicle in front, so that if it is forced to brake hard the following driver has time to react as well.

Fraudsters often disable brake lights on their vehicles to give the unsuspecting victim no chance of stopping in time, or use decoy vehicles that distract the innocent driver or force it to change lanes. The gang staging the crash will also often have 'independent' witnesses who conveniently happened to be present, apparently by chance.

The IFB says the crash for cash scam is a nationwide phenomenon and is not confined to any particular postcodes or hotspots.

Drivers are increasingly installing small CCTV cameras on their dashboards to provide evidence in their own favour. Your insurer may lower your premium if you do this, because it helps to save you from false claims.

Ghost of a chance

Not all crash for cash scams involve other drivers. Sometimes the criminals stage a crash between two vehicles they own, enhancing the damage with a crowbar or sledgehammer.

Better still from the fraudsters' point of view is the ghost accident, which involves submitting completely fabricated claims for accidents that never actually took place, and in some cases for cars that don't even exist.

Fraudsters look to make as much money out of the scam as possible. Each 'accident' can net anything up to £30,000 through a combination of exaggerated insurance claims for:

- Vehicle damage

- Personal injury
- Loss of earnings
- Bogus passenger claims
- Vehicle recovery
- Vehicle storage
- Car hire

In some cases bogus passengers are added to the claims list, suffering from injuries such as whiplash.

In Britain whiplash makes up 80% of motor injury claims, compared with 47% in Germany and only 3% in France. Whiplash claims rose by 62% between 2000 and 2013 in the UK, yet there was a 30% fall in accidents.

In France, injury claims fell by 55% in line with the decrease in road accidents and they have also fallen heavily in Germany, along with accident numbers.

Insurance company Aviva says that whiplash claims are at record levels and they add £93 to the average motor insurance premium of £372. The bill is rising as more claims pour in.

Insurers also incur expense in asking independent claims adjudicators to check that garages are not inflating claims.

Professional enablers

The reason why gangs rather than individuals are involved in crash for cash scams is that a fair amount of authentic paperwork is required to assess the losses suffered. For each element of loss presented, the fraudsters require the necessary paperwork from a professional to validate their claim.

Criminal gangs rely on key individuals and organisations such as recovery and storage companies, motor engineers, car repair body shops, hire car companies, doctors and solicitors, known collectively as 'professional enablers'. Some professionals may themselves be innocent dupes. Less scrupulous ones will be part of the scam, taking a fee for their services.

Claims management companies (CMCs) exist to take care of the needs of accident victims – everything from pursuing personal injury claims to arranging courtesy car hire while the damaged vehicle is being repaired. While many CMCs are genuine, some are set up by criminal gangs to assist them in their scams.

At the bottom of the chain are recruited drivers and passengers, whose lives are put at risk along with those of innocent motorists. Recruits can be willing participants or vulnerable members of society intimidated into assisting the scam. Since they are involved in the accident and need to give their names and addresses, they often carry the greatest risk of being caught first.

Among fraudsters convicted was a consultant motor engineer charged with 11 counts of conspiracy to defraud after he was recruited into a gang to write false vehicle reports for damage that had not occurred and for vehicles he had not even seen. In one case an insurance company paid out £7,810 for a vehicle he declared written off although it transpired he never actually saw it.

Members of the public can report crash for cash fraud anonymously through the Insurance Fraud Bureau Cheatline on 0800 422 0421 or its website: www.insurancefraudbureau.org.

Other insurance scams

The crash for cash scam is part of a wider pattern of false claims, including on home and other insurance. Each day insurers uncover 381 fraudulent insurance claims costing more than £2.7 million. That's 2,670 fraudulent claims a week.

Trust me, I'm an official

You get a telephone call from someone who claims to be an officer at some sort of transport agency. It all sounds very official and you get the impression you are talking to some government or police agency.

The 'officer' understands that someone at this address was involved in a road accident in the past three years and he is just checking the file before closing it. Has everything been resolved or should he keep the file open?

It may well be that you have not had an accident. You say no and the call is terminated. However, there are on average nearly 200,000 accidents a year on British roads in which someone is killed or injured so there will be a fair proportion of people answering the call who have indeed been involved in a road accident, whether as a driver, passenger or pedestrian.

By making it sound as if he is keeping official records, the scammer may bluff you into giving full details about yourself and your vehicle, including the registration number and your insurance company, plus details of any other driver involved.

The person ringing you is NOT an official and he is NOT in charge of police or Department of Transport records. You are not obliged to give him any information.

Accident management companies

Your details will be sold on to an accident management company that will try to persuade you to let them take up a claim on your behalf. Such companies can operate entirely legally and legitimately, but the ethical ones will not be employing ambulance chasers to drum up trade.

You may find yourself accepting a 'free' courtesy car or embarking on expensive medical treatment under the impression that the other party will be paying. If the other party disputes liability, you will end up bearing the expense yourself. Worse still, the details you provided may be used to support a claim against you by the other party. Scammers don't care whose side they are on.

If you cannot be persuaded to put the phone down on the scammer and you are foolish enough to get sucked into an insurance claim, do not think of exaggerating any expenses or injury you have suffered, even if the accident management company encourages you to do so.

If the case goes to court you will be forced to commit perjury, a serious offence, or admit you were trying to defraud the other party's insurance company.

How insurance scams have changed

- Insurance has become more impersonal, with fewer policies sold through an agent who knows the client. This has made ordinary, law abiding citizens more willing to bend the rules.

- The growth in the number of drivers on the road has meant that claims have burgeoned in number, making it easier to hide bogus claims among the genuine ones.

- Scammers are now organised into gangs with members who can back up each other's claims.

How we can beat the scammers

It's harder for members of the general public to fight this scam as it's the insurance industry in the firing line. However, we can all play our part by reporting any insurance scams we become aware of.

If you are involved in an accident, try to get as much information as possible from anyone else who is involved and take photographs of the scene, including any damage. Write down any details while you remember them. Do not agree to falsify any details.

Beware of cheap insurance deals from any company you have never heard of.

Traditional scams summary

We can see there are reoccurring themes that come up in these traditional scams. Knowing how to spot them and how to respond can help you avoid being a victim:

- Don't be greedy
- Don't bite when something looks too good to be true
- Don't indulge in anything that is or might be illegal
- Don't trust complete strangers
- Don't rush into anything
- Do consult people you know and trust

*   *   *

In Section B we look at investment scams and seeing how these basic principles apply in that area too.

SECTION B.
INVESTMENT SCAMS

CHAPTER 10.
The Risks Of Investing

INVESTING IS A SENSIBLE WAY OF PREPARING FOR THE FUTURE has in store for us and, ultimately, a comfortable old age. As with everything in life, it has its risks, and unsophisticated investors are a target for scammers.

Some investments are traded on a properly regulated exchange where there are trading rules, participants must put up cash before they can invest and prices are set by supply and demand. Trading is held on all weekdays except public holidays.

Shares are an obvious example, provided you trade on a properly regulated stock market such as the London Stock Exchange or similar institutions in New York, Europe and many Asian countries. Gold is also traded on formal exchanges using prices that are published in the press so you know where you stand.

The importance of these exchanges is that they effectively guarantee that you will be able to sell your investments at a fair price if you choose to cash in. Competition between brokers ensures that trading costs are kept to a minimum.

Properly regulated stock exchanges have made strenuous efforts over the past couple of decades to stamp out abuses that favour a few insiders over the many small investors without access to privileged information.

Among such measures are:

- All information that may affect a company's share price must be put into the public domain as soon as possible.

- Company results are released an hour before the start of trading so everyone has a chance to see them (there are exceptions for companies listed on two exchanges in different time zones).

- Directors are not allowed to buy or sell shares in their own company ahead of results announcements.

- Takeover approaches must be confirmed or denied once rumours start to circulate and any bid must be conducted in an orderly fashion, with all shareholders treated equally.

- Buying or selling shares using information received as an insider that has not been released to the public is a criminal offence.

It is extremely difficult to stamp out malpractice altogether, even on a well-regulated exchange. The temptation for quick, certain profits will always be a strong pull and too many people need to know about events behind the scenes to stop the unscrupulous from taking advantage.

For many investments, though, there not even the protection of a regulated exchange. This is the case with antiques, collectibles and fine arts, where you trade through dealers and auction houses and where charges and the spread between buying and selling prices can be substantial.

Valuation is extremely difficult, as any television viewers familiar with the wave of antiques and collectibles programmes shown on television most afternoons will be aware. Even the experts can be wildly out in their estimates. Much depends on the condition of the items sold, who happens to be in the auction room and what type of goods are in fashion.

In this section we will look at various investment scams. Before we do so, here are some general pointers that will help you to avoid falling victim to them.

How to avoid investment scams

- Buy and sell through a respected and well-regulated exchange if one exists. Otherwise use well-known and reputable dealers.

- Do not buy complex investments from complete strangers, especially those who cold call.

- Do not invest in anything you do not understand.

- Be prepared to walk away from an investment, even if you miss a potentially attractive buying opportunity.

- Check whether there is a reasonable certainty that you will be able to sell the asset(s) when you want to cash in.

- Where possible use a payment system where you can cancel the deal and get your money back if it turns out to be a con.

- Take advantage of any cooling-off period, if one exists, to reconsider whether you have made a wise investment.

- If you have nagging doubts, do not commit to an investment without stepping back to think about it.

- The more pressure someone puts you under to make an investment, the more suspicious you should be.

- If you are conned, do not throw good money after bad trying to rescue your investment.

You should also remember that the value of your investments can go down, although if you stick to properly regulated trading their worth is unlikely to drop to zero unless you are very unlucky and very careless. The important point to remember with investing is that the greater the potential reward, the greater the risk you are likely to be taking.

Let's now move on to look at the scams themselves in more detail.

CHAPTER 11.
Rumour Scams

THERE IS NO SUCH THING AS AN ABSOLUTELY RISK-FREE investment, yet that has not stopped the foolhardy and the gullible from throwing money at companies ranging from speculative to downright bizarre in the belief that nothing can possibly go wrong.

Stock market investing has, though, come a long way since the worst excesses of the early 1700s, when the concept of buying and selling shares was in its infancy and London was developing as an investment centre.

Then all manner of companies suddenly sprang up, ranging from ludicrously optimistic to downright fraudulent. One company that floated said its intention was to buy the Irish bogs and another proposed to manufacture a gun to fire square cannon balls. The most ridiculous and blatantly suspect operation was "For carrying-on an undertaking of great advantage but no-one to know what it is." This attracted £2,000 from investors.

Stuffing your ears

Aficionados of William Shakespeare will be well acquainted with Rumour, the character who opens King Henry IV, Part 2 by "stuffing the ears of men with false reports."

However well regulated a stock market is, there will always be scope for false rumours that drive share prices higher or lower. Some turn out to be true, or partly true, while others are pure speculation or deliberately misleading. Active share traders can make small fortunes from trading on rumours and getting out before the truth emerges.

On the whole, it is better to ignore a rumour and miss an opportunity than it is to invest and get caught out. Indeed, this is a good general rule for all approaches that you suspect to be scams: better to risk missing out than risk being mugged.

The du Bourg hoax

Less than 100 years after the infamous South Sea Bubble of 1720, but long enough for memories to fade and a new generation of investors to emerge ready to be scalped, one of the greatest rumour scams was hatched. As in Shakespeare's play, this rumour spread news of the death of a war leader which, had it been true, would have had profound consequences.

A man dressed in military uniform and claiming to be Colonel du Bourg, aide-de-camp to Lord Cathcart, arrived at the Ship Inn at Dover on a Monday morning in February 1814. He claimed that French leader Napoleon Bonaparte had been killed and thus the war between Britain and France was over, with the Bourbon monarchy restored in France.

It is easy to see why the rumour was believed:

- Dover was the nearest UK port to France and it was thus reasonable for du Bourg to land there as he raced to bring the glad tidings to London.

- People wanted to believe the story because the war had dragged on at considerable expense, with Britain subsidising its Austrian and Russian allies. The national debt had soared and Napoleon had closed European markets to British exports.

- Napoleon had been seriously weakened by his invasion of Russia and his subsequent retreat from Moscow when his forces were ravaged by cold and hunger.

- Rumours of Napoleon's defeat had already been circulating.

Du Bourg arranged for the information to be relayed to the Admiralty in London and he himself headed in that direction, stopping at inns to repeat his story.

Market impact

As the news from Dover began to circulate among traders on the London Stock Exchange, the value of government and other stocks soared.

When the market began to falter around midday on the lack of official confirmation, the buying frenzy was reignited by the appearance of three men dressed as French officers in Bourbon uniforms celebrating in London and proclaiming the restoration of the Bourbons.

However, the entire affair was a deliberate hoax. In the afternoon, the government confirmed that the news of peace was a fabrication and government stocks fell back sharply.

Heads must roll

There was little doubt that someone had made a packet from deliberate stock manipulation and the London Stock Exchange soon set up a committee to investigate who the guilty parties were.

The committee found that on the day of the false rumour more than £1.1 million worth of two government-based stocks had been sold. Most of it had been bought only the previous week when prices were lower, so the sellers had made a quick, hefty profit.

Three people implicated in the purchase and sale were charged with fraud. They were Lord Cochrane, his uncle the Honourable Andrew Cochrane-Johnstone and Richard Butt, Lord Cochrane's financial advisor. Captain Random de Berenger, a fast mover who had posed as du Bourg and then apparently managed to get to London in time to dress up as a French Bourbon officer, was also arrested.

The chief conspirators were found guilty and sentenced to 12 months in prison, fined £1,000 each and made to spend an hour in the public pillory; a somewhat fitting punishment, substituting one set of stocks for another.

At the bar of public opinion

Then, as now, it was not easy to nail the guilty parties. Lord Cochrane, who despite his title was a member of the House of Commons, protested his innocence and such was his popularity that he was spared the ordeal of the pillory for fear that it would lead to a riot.

He was subsequently re-elected as an MP but it took until 1832 for him to be granted a free pardon, including reinstatement to his rank of Rear Admiral. Restoration of the Order of the Bath and other honours followed.

Modern rumours

Perhaps the most spectacular untrue rumour of modern times was a false report that social website Twitter had received a $31 billion takeover approach. The story was published in July 2015 on the internet using the same background and style as international news service Bloomberg, so it was widely believed. The name of a genuine Bloomberg reporter was used in the byline.

Making the hoax easier for traders to swallow was that Twitter had often been surrounded by stories speculating that it could be the subject of a takeover bid from other internet companies such as Google. Twitter's shares jumped 8% within minutes.

The fake website masquerading as Bloomberg turned out to have been registered in Panama five days earlier. The article, citing "people with knowledge of the situation," said Twitter was "working closely with bankers after receiving an offer to be bought out for $31 billion."

A genuine Twitter account closely followed by traders picked up the story, giving it wider publicity.

Bloomberg acted quickly in denying that it had published the report, yet even so Twitter's stock ended the day at £36.72, which was 2.6% higher than the previous night's close.

Only two months earlier shares of cosmetics group Avon soared after a news release was filed with the Securities and Exchange Commission, the US financial regulator, claiming that it was the target of a takeover bid from a fictitious company named as PTG Capital. The filing mimicked announcements made by genuine private-equity firm TPG.

The SEC later said in a lawsuit that the false Avon report came from a 37-year-old man in Bulgaria. The suit said that the man had manipulated stocks in a similar fashion on two previous occasions over four years.

In another unusual development, shares of Penn Virginia spiked after a news outlet reported that the US energy producer had rejected an $8-a-share takeover offer from British oil major BP. People familiar with the companies said no such offer or rejection occurred between them.

That report appears to have gained traction due to documentation still available online from the same date 13 years earlier of a previous takeover tussle involving Penn Virginia and a suitor with a name similar to BP's.

How the rumour scam has changed over the years

The basic idea of buying shares, driving up the price then selling at a profit is unchanged, but the sheer amount of information, comment and opinion that courses through markets makes it difficult for traders operating at high speeds to avoid a well-crafted hoax.

Trading volumes are much greater and far more companies have their shares quoted on major exchanges, so there is more scope to manipulate trading.

Many professional traders use computer programmes to decide when to buy and sell, so sharp movements in share prices are magnified as programmes operate stop losses, which are signals that traders should sell falling shares to limit their losses.

What we can do to beat the scammers

Well-run stock exchanges have rules to minimise the scope for false rumours. Where shares move sharply a company is obliged to say whether there is any reason for the movement. All information that could materially affect shares prices must be put in the public domain as widely and as quickly as possible. Companies must also produce accounts and trading updates at least twice a year.

However, it will never be possible for the exchanges or financial regulators to stamp out rumours entirely. Investors for their part should be extremely wary of shares in any company that move sharply for no obvious reason. By the time you hear the rumour you have almost certainly missed the best chance to buy anyway.

Ways that we can protect ourselves are:

- Be wary of any stock market rumour you have no means of verifying.

- If shares in a particular company have already risen strongly on a rumour, accept that you have already missed the best buying opportunity.

We now move on to supposed stock market opportunities where ordinary investors seemed to be offered the chance to get ahead of the game rather than react to events outside their control.

CHAPTER 12.
Tip For Tap Scams

THERE IS A SAYING IN THE STOCK MARKET, "WHERE THERE'S a tip, there's a tap." In plainer English, when someone offers you a hot tip they are probably directly or indirectly tapping you for cash. Your decision to buy is someone else's opportunity to sell.

There is nothing illegal about share tipping as such. Tips appear daily in several respectable newspapers. You are charged nothing for these tips apart from the price of the newspaper and the papers themselves have nothing to lose or gain, other than their reputation, whether you make a successful investment or not.

Many investors willingly pay a subscription to receive suggestions and recommendations from stockbrokers. That's fine provided the broker is registered with the FCA and is providing properly researched advice.

It is also possible to subscribe to tip sheets. Here the waters get a little murkier. Whatever claims they make for how well their tips have done, you have to take their word for it. As a general rule, the greater the claims of success, the larger the pinch of salt you should take with them. Remember that no one, not even the most successful professionals, gets it right all the time and if they are making so much money for themselves why are they bothering to share their expertise with you?

Whenever you are shown performance figures remember that even if these are genuine they will be highly selective or will have been manipulated to produce the desired effect.

Danger signs are:

- Tips and systems accompanied by mouth-watering claims of success

- Unsolicited share tips by phone or email

- Complex trading systems you don't understand

- Cherry picking of performance figures

One of the most common and dangerous tip for tap scams is the boiler room scam.

The boiler room scam

Boiler rooms employ salesmen to cold call potential investors and use high-pressure sales techniques to talk their victims into buying stocks or other assets of low or non-existent value. Rather worryingly, they seem able to target people who have already bought genuine investments, which suggests that names and contact numbers are being sold on.

Like a pack of wolves

Salesmen can be extremely persistent and persuasive, relying on wearing down the resistance of their targets. Their tactics and techniques are brilliantly captured by the main character in the book *The Wolf of Wall Street*, played in the film of the same name by Leonardo DiCaprio, in which a failed stockbroker makes a fortune selling worthless shares at inflated prices.

The salesmen are well briefed on the investments they are offering, able to quote facts and figures about the companies they are pushing, how well previous investments have done and the mouth-watering profits that earlier investors have made.

Boiler rooms may have impressive looking websites loaded with gushing comments from 'satisfied customers'. They are often, though not always, based abroad, out of the reach of regulatory authorities.

Chairs are for bears

'Chairs are for bears' was the infamous motto of a company called Harvard Securities, possibly the most notorious boiler room operation. Bears as in the stock market sense of pessimists – that is people who give up because they don't expect to succeed. So the Harvard Securities dealing room had no chairs, just telephones.

Salespeople (almost always men) were more likely to make a sale standing up rather than enjoying the comfort of a chair.

The company collapsed in 1988 after failing to receive authorisation by financial regulators and being turned down for membership of the London Stock Exchange after an inquiry into its operations by the Department of Trade and Industry. The collapse left thousands of investors out of pocket and unable to sell the illiquid shares they had been pressurised into buying.

The man behind Harvard Securities, Tom Wilmot, trained the salesmen not to be put off by a string of 'not interested' replies. They were told to "tell your story often enough and you cannot help but make sales. As you acquire more experience you will find it easier and easier to meet and overcome objections."

This was so successful that the business was turning over more than £200 million a year when it collapsed. Wilmot left the UK for almost eight years while he negotiated the settlement of a multi-million pound tax liability with HM Revenue & Customs but he returned in 2001 and set up another boiler room scam with operations in Spain and eastern Europe.

It was not until 2011 that his actions finally caught up with him and he was sentenced at to nine years in jail for conspiracy to defraud investors out of £27.5 million through boiler rooms.

How they operate

Boiler rooms will push investments in foreign companies, diamonds, carbon credits, land, rare and precious metals – anything that their victims will have limited knowledge of, but which seem to offer the possibility of spectacular gains.

Ask yourself these questions:

- Why have you been selected to receive this hot news?

- Why are the people offering this investment opportunity not snapping it up themselves and making a killing?

- Is the person ringing, and the company he works for, regulated? If so, by whom?

- Are they regulated to recommend or sell investments in this country?

- How can this person possibly know what your investment needs are, how much you can safely invest and what degree of risk you are willing to take?

- Who says this investment is underpriced? Has it been valued independently and by whom?

- Do you really know anything about the asset on offer?

- How will you be able to sell the asset to take your profit?

Remember, you should be asking yourself these questions. You ask the stranger on the phone at your peril. He may well have glib and convincing answers that will suck you in. Once you start showing an interest you are only encouraging him to apply more pressure and wear you down.

Inside information

Providing inside information to selected people is against the rules of respectable stock exchanges and in many countries, including the UK and US, it is illegal to act on such information.

If you buy shares on what is supposed to be inside information you will have no comeback if that information turns out to be false and you lose money on any investment you made. Are you going to go to the authorities and complain that you were cheated when acting on what you thought was inside information? Not likely, as you have broken the law yourself.

You can buy but not sell

The chances are, though, that any shares or assets on offer are not traded on a properly regulated exchange. If you buy, you will subsequently find that it is nigh on impossible to sell these supposedly sought-after investments.

Companies on offer tend to be:

- Mining or natural resources companies producing raw materials that are genuinely in demand.

- Impressively named.

- Based abroad where you are unlikely to have specialist knowledge.

- Without a trading record that you can study.

The fact that the shares are not quoted means that you have no marketplace to sell them. You are stuck until the company joins a stock market – and that is probably not going to happen. You can't sell the shares back to the cold caller because, even if you have some means of contacting him, he flatly refuses to buy them back – unless you agree to buy a larger stake in yet another unquoted company.

The cold caller will be able to contact you, though. He will do so over and over again with more and more share tips that cannot possibly go wrong. He knows a mug when he finds one.

Things get nasty

These people keep coming back until you have no money left. Victims have lost their entire life savings, damaged their health and ended up in hospital as a result of the stress.

If you try to drop out, boiler rooms can turn extremely unpleasant. There have been reports of boiler rooms:

- Demanding VAT on top of money you have already invested.

- Claiming that you are in breach of contract unless you pay more.

- Claiming that you have been referred to the fraud squad.

- Threatening to have you prosecuted for being abusive to their staff.

- Giving the impression that the person calling you is a police officer.

- Threatening to visit you at home.

There is only one sensible course of action you can take and that is to put the phone down. Only deal with stockbrokers that you approach, not those who approach you.

Don't hand over your money to someone you don't know for something you haven't seen and don't really know anything about.

How tip for tap scams have changed over the years

- The development of modern communications has made it easier for boiler rooms to contact victims.
- Greater affluence has produced richer pickings.
- The burgeoning elderly population means there are more vulnerable people to bully.

How we can beat the scammers

- Never invest money with a cold caller.
- Put the phone down immediately or delete the email when a complete stranger tries to sell you investments.
- Invest only through properly regulated exchanges or trading platforms.

The point about a growing elderly population being targeted takes us neatly on to consider the ease with which the elderly can be parted from their hard-earned pension pots.

CHAPTER 13.
Pensions Scams

IN HIS 2015 BUDGET, CHANCELLOR OF THE EXCHEQUER George Osborne announced that people approaching retirement age would be allowed to draw cash out of their private pension pots. He argued that people should be trusted with their own money.

However, give anyone a lump sum and they are liable to squander at least part of it. Such measures also open the door to scammers who are adept at parting people from their cash.

Pension freedom changes

Osborne's first move was to allow people over the age of 55 to draw money out of their pension pots, with any withdrawal up to 25% of the total pot tax free. This facility will be available for the under-55s when they reach that age. Most people who have already retired were excluded, but anyone with a drawdown pension – one where they still have the right to withdraw cash from the pot – could also benefit from the new arrangements.

When this went down well, the Chancellor went one step further with plans to allow those who had already retired to sell their annuities.

The moves have two main drawbacks:

- People are likely to spend the money foolishly and will thus be more dependent on the state pension and other benefits later on.

- Scammers will be waiting to pounce on those looking for ways to invest their cash.

According to official Treasury predictions, half a million people would seek access to their pension savings. That is a lot of people lining up to potentially make ill-informed decisions.

To make matters worse, in a previous and unrelated move, changes to charges that independent financial advisers can make have unintentionally reduced the scope for investors to seek advice. No longer able to charge commission, many IFAs packed up, some high street banks exited the advisory market and a high number of advisory firms now offer only restricted advice.

Many remaining IFAs will only consider advising those with more than £50,000 to invest. So those who need advice about how to invest their funds may have difficulty in obtaining it.

Pension industry experts think that any cash withdrawn will be used in three ways, split fairly evenly:

1. **Squandered**. The only reason why you saved for a pension was because you had to be in the company scheme. Now you can get hold of the cash you can blow it on a Caribbean cruise, a new car or designer clothes.

2. **Home improvements**. Building that conservatory you always wanted, modernising the bathroom or redecorating throughout. At least you will have some lasting benefit from

this and you are likely to spend more time at home when you are retired.

3. **Investment**. Using your pension pot for its intended purpose: to provide comfort in your old age.

With pensions you need to think long term, whatever your age. You may be retired for a long time. Women in the UK who reach pension age have a 50-50 chance of living to 90. Men, who tend to live shorter lives, have a one-third chance of reaching 90 once they have crossed the pension threshold.

So investments should be solid, perhaps boring, and designed to grow in value to offset the ravages of inflation. That, however, is pretty unexciting. Many investors will be keen to squander some of their cash and try to place the rest in higher yielding but riskier investments.

The knives are out

What has happened in the pensions revolution demonstrates the thin line that sometimes exists between legal sharp practice and outright scams. Pension providers were soon being accused of imposing high fees for early withdrawal, as they were entitled to do. This was not exactly a scam but those losing out might have felt that way.

Secondly, scammers inevitably descend on anyone coming unexpectedly into money. They were soon concocting schemes that purported to offer far greater returns than annuities. Those reaching retirement age would be well advised to be extremely cautious if anyone contacts them asking them to sell their annuity, and they should not allow themselves to be rushed into making a decision they are likely to regret.

Scammers were already at work even before their victims were allowed to legitimately lay their own hands on their pension pots. Lists of people aged 55 and over were being sold for 5p per person. Some lists went to genuine advisers but too many organisations will happily sell a list to whoever is willing to pay for it, no questions asked.

Hard come, easy go

Pensions are built up over a lifetime but can be squandered in seconds. According to life fund specialist Phoenix Group, there was a three-fold increase in pension scams between the point of the changes being announced and when they came into effect. The main opening tactic was to offer a free pension review or free government guidance to help people take advantage of the reforms.

When it all goes wrong, victims will be unable to claim compensation from the Financial Services Compensation Scheme (FSCS) or take their case to the Financial Ombudsman. Nor can pension providers save you from yourself by stopping you transferring your entitlement into bogus schemes.

Some scammers were content to punt bogus schemes for getting better returns than were available from pensions providers. Some offers were quite eye-catching. But, as ever, the bigger the prospective return, the less likely it is to materialise.

Stunts pulled included investing in student accommodation in Nigeria returning 28% (someone learnt a lesson from Goebbels), bamboo, car parks, storage units, graphene and carbon credits. As these are all unregulated investments there is nothing to stop the scammers from promising the moon in marketing material. Other scammers widened their horizons by pedalling schemes such as renewable energy installations that were too good to be true – although people believed them anyway.

One line was to tell victims that their pension pot wasn't big enough to provide a worthwhile income. So why not spend it on double glazing or cavity wall installation that would pay for itself in double quick time? How about solar panels or pumps for extracting heat from below ground? Other offers include repaving drives or garden landscaping; schemes that are money straight down the drain with little pretence of being a decent investment.

You're never too young...

The FCA found that scammers were even targeting people who had not yet reached the age of 55. Any withdrawals they make would be subject to 55% tax.

To make matters worse, scammers are perfectly capable of cloning a financial adviser's website, complete with FCA registration number and address, to look authentic.

They will use phrases such as "loophole", "free pension review" and "ethical investment" to lure the unsuspecting. Loopholes rarely exist for anyone other than the rich and free reviews usually turn out to be extremely expensive.

... and never too old

Even before pensions freedom day in April 2015, Age UK, the charity for older people, found in a survey that 53% of those polled realised they had been on the receiving end of an attempted scam. This could easily be an underrepresentation – it is reasonable to expect that almost all elderly people have been targeted, but many may not have realised it.

About 70% of those who realised they had been targeted admitted they had lost money but most did not bother reporting the crime.

Age UK fears that older people will be targeted increasingly by fraudsters, especially as they are gradually using the internet more.

Tactics include:

- Befriending and grooming lonely victims.

- Isolating victims from friends and relatives.

- Using documentation and websites that look professional and official.

- Impersonating financial advisers, banks and police.

- Issuing threats and using intimidation.

- Taking advantage of those suffering from dementia.

You can check on pension scams by visiting the website of The Pensions Regulator (**www.thepensionsregulator.gov.uk/pension-scams**).

How we can beat the scammers

- Beware of people who approach you out of the blue.

- Talk to people you know before investing your pension pot.

- Don't rush into an investment – you've saved for a lifetime so don't squander the money in seconds.

- Beware of callers who claim, or give the impression, that they are government advisers. The government is NOT offering advice on how to reinvest your pension.

Now let's look at some of the other investment scams that offer scope for deceit.

CHAPTER 14.
Art Scams

THERE IS SOMETHING ABOUT THE WORLD OF ART THAT presents a special challenge to scammers. Some of the ingredients are:

- Even experts can disagree on whether a painting is genuine.

- Experts also sometimes disagree on whether a famous artist or a pupil painted the picture.

- We all dream of finding a masterpiece in the attic.

- Many of us kid ourselves that we could spot the real thing.

- Artists and styles come in and out of fashion so timing can be important.

- Today's mocked artist can be tomorrow's genius.

The man who fooled Hermann Göring

One of the most famous forgers of all time was Dutch artist Han van Meegeren, who was so desperate to be recognised as a legitimate artist that he started painting in the style of Johannes Vermeer.

Van Meegeren proved his point. His paintings were so good that buyers thought they really were by Vermeer. At one point he sold six of his fakes for a total reputed to be about £40 million. His most successful forgery was Supper at Emmaus, which he created in 1937 while living in the south of France. This painting was hailed by some of the world's foremost art experts as the finest Vermeer they had ever seen.

He came unstuck when, during the second world war, one of his paintings ended up in the collection of Hermann Göring, the Nazi Reichsmarschall. Göring would have done well to consult his colleague Goebbels, who knew all about big lies.

At the end of the war, van Meegeren was arrested as a collaborator, accused of selling Dutch cultural property to the Nazis. This would have been an act of treason, carrying the death penalty, so van Meegeren had little choice but to confess that he had painted the picture himself as a forgery. Van Meegeren was convicted of forgery and sentenced to a year in prison, although he died of a heart attack before he could serve it.

Death before dishonour

The Hungarian painter Elmyr de Hory also paid with his life when his past as a forger came to light during an art fraud investigation in 1976. He committed suicide rather than face the consequences of selling about 1,000 forged works from renowned artists such as Modigliani, Degas, Picasso and Matisse.

Like van Meergeren, he had to be a pretty good artist to get away with it and since his death his pieces have become sought after in their own right.

Nothing is sacred

There are many more stories of forgers who got away with it, at least for some considerable time. British artist John Myatt completed around 200 forgeries of artists such as Matisse, Picasso, Monet and Renoir. Some were sold at respected auction house including Phillips, Sotheby's and Christie's.

He was arrested by Scotland Yard in 1995 and served a year in jail. On his release he continued to paint and he later starred in a TV series where he shared some of his secrets on copying other people's artwork.

In Bolton, Lancashire, Shaun Greenhalgh, along with his 84-year old father George and 83-year-old mother Olive, forged sculptures, paintings and rare artefacts for 17 years. Their output included replicas of works by L. S. Lowry, Barbara Hepworth and Paul Gauguin. Their crowning glory was fooling the Bolton Museum into purchasing a fake Egyptian sculpture, the Amarna Princess, that experts believed dated back to 1350 BC.

Attributing artworks and detecting forgeries is made much more difficult by the fact that experts change their minds. For example, the Fitzwilliam Museum in Cambridge suddenly announced that a pair of pretty Renaissance bronzes ascribed to an unknown hand were now thought to be the work of Michelangelo. Upgradings don't come bigger than that.

The art loan scam

Few of us will be caught out paying hundreds of thousands of pounds for a fake painting or sculpture, but we could get caught in a scam involving the loan of expensive paintings. This sophisticated fraud has had a limited run but it is worth relating because it has important lessons for the unsuspecting. It goes like this:

The fraudster offers you the opportunity to buy a painting for £10,000 that can be hired out for £1,000 a year. You are told that high-class restaurants prefer to hire paintings so that the decor can be refreshed regularly. It is thus cheaper for them to hire paintings for a set period rather than keep buying new ones. A return of 10% on any investment is very tempting. It means that you have got all your money back in ten years and you will still have ownership of a painting that will increase in value.

You are naturally doubtful. However, your doubts are assuaged by an assurance that the caller is so certain a 10% return can be achieved, he will guarantee the first three years' lettings himself before sending you the painting at the end of the third year.

You part with your money under intense sales pressure and suffer an uneasy 12 months. Oh ye of little faith! At the end of the first year a cheque arrives for £1,000. Hallelujah! It was genuine after all.

So you waste no time in boasting to your friends about your financial acumen. Perhaps you recruit one or two of them to make a similar investment. Thus you become the recruiting officer for the scheme, which saves the scammers from having to bother. Where is the drawback?

You think that you have made £1,000. Yet you started with £10,000 and you now have £1,000, so in fact you are currently £9,000 down! In your euphoria at discovering what a brilliant investor you are you overlook these basic points:

- The scammer has returned £1,000 of your own money, having had the use of your £10,000 for the past year.

- The scammer still has £9,000 of your cash.

- You have no idea whether the painting actually exists.

- If it does exist, who painted it and what is it called?

- Who has valued the painting at £10,000?

- Which restaurant has supposedly been displaying the painting and where will it hang in the second year?

Even if you do think to ask you will be stonewalled unless you insist on answers and then you will have difficulty in checking any information supplied.

When, at the end of the second year, you receive another £1,000 you are further reassured and at the end of the third year you may well receive a final £1,000, plus a painting delivered to your door.

You will soon find that restaurants have not the least interest in hiring your painting, and certainly not at £1,000 a year. There is no point in complaining to the scammer, who has a ready response: "I kept my side of the bargain. I managed to hire out the painting. You're not trying hard enough or going to the right restaurants."

Belatedly, you may have the painting valued independently. It will be worth perhaps £1,000. The upshot is that you lost the use of £10,000 for three years and are still £6,000 out of pocket.

To add insult to injury, you have recruited your friends into the scam. They will find out what sort of financial brain you have when their three-year terms come to an end.

There are some simple lessons here that can be applied beyond this particular scam:

- Do not get sucked into investment schemes by complete strangers.

- Don't feel you have been left out when friends boast about great schemes they have joined.

- Always look for a catch in any investment idea – and look hard. The drawback may not be obvious.

- Be particularly wary of any scheme that offers guaranteed high returns, as there is likely to be a catch.

- Talk about any proposal with friends, particularly any that have financial acumen, asking if they can spot the flaw.

- It is better to walk away and miss out on a 10% return than to fall for a scam and lose 100% of your money.

CHAPTER 15.
The Auction Ring Scam

ORDINARY PEOPLE HAVE BEEN ENCOURAGED TO TAKE part in auctions by the many television programmes in which family heirlooms and items hidden away in the attic have proved to be quite valuable. You do not have to be an expert to sell at auction, since the bidding sets the price. You need to know what you are doing only when you are buying. Auctions have grown increasingly popular for this reason.

Auctions are particularly popular for the following items:

- Antiques.

- Collectibles – such as stamps, coins, vintage toys, classic cars and fine art.

- Fine wines.

- Property.

- House clearances.

- Goods seized in insolvencies.

When you sell goods at an auction you enter something of a lottery. You need only two people who desperately want the item to enter into a bidding war for the price to be bid up to a level beyond your wildest dreams. If only one person in the room is keen you are doomed to disappointment. The sum you receive will be far below the price that the bidder was prepared to pay had there been competing bids.

Matters are made far worse if a group of buyers at an auction collude not to bid against each other in order to keep the auction price low. Such a group is known in the trade as a ring.

One member of the ring bids on a lot while the others abstain. They will re-auction among themselves any goods bought at the first auction. The difference between what the successful bidder paid and the proceeds of the second, private auction, are distributed among the group.

Operating or participating in a ring is illegal in the UK under several laws. It fraudulently distorts competition in the auction room, deprives the seller of the true value of their property and has a detrimental effect on the level of the auctioneer's commission.

Offenders risk a fine and up to five years imprisonment. They may be prohibited from taking part in future auctions or acting as a company director for a number of years. The original seller is entitled to annul the original sale to the ring member and demand compensation – provided they find out about it.

The laws

The Auction (Bidding Agreements) Acts of 1927 and 1969 make it a criminal offence for dealers to give an inducement or reward to any person for abstaining from bidding at a sale by auction. It is also an offence for dealers to accept the inducement or reward.

It is not, however, an offence for two or more people to agree to bid jointly. This can be useful if an expensive asset such as a house is auctioned and none of the joint bidders could afford to buy it on their own. If you are in this position, make sure that you and the other parties have a signed agreement to this effect and that a copy of the agreement is lodged with the auctioneer before the auction.

The Enterprise Act of 2002 makes it a criminal offence to participate in a bid-rigging arrangement under which one or more potential bidders abstain from bidding or bid in a pre-agreed way.

Competition law in the UK includes the provisions of the EC Treaty (where there is a potential effect on trade between member states) and the Competition Act 1998. The Competition Act prohibits agreements, decisions or concerted practices between undertakings which have as their object or effect the prevention, restriction or distortion of competition within the UK.

The problem is proving it. These agreements are naturally made in private and none of the participants are likely to blab. The presence of several dealers at an auction, each bidding for different items, can look perfectly normal. There have been only a handful of prosecutions under the Auction Acts.

If you sell at an auction you will naturally look for one near to home, otherwise travelling costs eat up any gain from going further afield. If the item is very valuable it is worth going to one of the bigger auction houses; although charges will be higher it brings credibility and a wider reach.

Otherwise try to pick a large local auction that lots of people attend so bidding is more competitive. Many auctioneers have assistants taking bids over the telephone or online, which increases the potential reach.

Tables turned

Buyers may seek to turn the tables by bidding the price up themselves. A buyer who has set a reserve price – the lowest price that he or she is prepared to accept – may feel justified in pushing the bidding up to that level, since any lower bids will be unsuccessful and the item will not be sold. This is of questionable morality and in Britain and many other countries bidding on one's own lot is illegal.

A bidding ring was used as the central plot in an episode of the British television series *Lovejoy*, in which the price of a watercolour by a fictional artist was inflated so that others by the same artist could be sold for more than their purchase price.

The danger is not just in the long arm of the law but the risk of being hoisted on your own petard. Your aim, naturally, is to drop out of the bidding just before it reaches a climax.

However, you have no way of knowing how far to push the other, genuine, bidder and you may end up making the highest bid when you could have sold for a decent price had you not been too greedy. You now have to pay the auctioneer's fee and the buyer's and seller's commission.

Chandelier or rafter bidding

Sometimes the auctioneer will help the bidding along by pretending there has been a higher bid. It is in the auctioneer's interests to extract the highest possible bid as he or she will earn more commission.

The auctioneer, like the seller, will not want the bidding to fall short of the reserve price and may raise false bids at crucial times to create the appearance that more people are interested in the item or to keep the momentum going.

He or she will quickly fix their gaze at a point in the auction room where it is difficult for the audience to see who is supposedly bidding, hence the name chandelier or rafter bidding given to this practice. It is also known as off-the-wall bidding.

With phone and internet bidding now commonplace it is easy to pretend that a higher bid has come in from a remote bidder. Only the auction room staff know what is said on the phone or the auctioneer's computer screen. Alternatively, a stooge may be placed in the audience to make bids in collusion with the auctioneer or vendor to deceive genuine bidders into paying more.

A word of advice to anyone tempted to cheat in this manner: don't even think about it. This is fraud.

Watch your goods

If you do sell by auction, try to keep an eye on your items while they are on display for would-be bidders to inspect before the auction. People can be quite unscrupulous.

Before an auction some bidders examine the lots and, in a loud voice in front of other potential bidders, cast doubt on the authenticity or quality of items that they intend to bid for. Rival bidders are scared off and they get the items they want cheaply.

Another trick, where there are several items in one lot, is to switch a rare item from one lot to another selection of much lower value. The dishonest bidder buys the cheaper batch and walks off with it before anyone realises. Bidders have also been known to switch lot numbers marking the items to produce the same effect.

Some people have even been known to steal part of a lot and then offer it for sale to the buyer of the lot after the auction to complete the set.

* * *

As we have noted at several points, modern technology has given a new twist to many traditional scams. In the final section we look at the scourges that can afflict anyone with a telephone and/or computer.

SECTION C.
MODERN SCAMS

CHAPTER 16.
How Technology Is Used

MODERN TECHNOLOGY HAS BEEN A WONDERFUL BOON to scammers. Although much of today's trickery is adapted from age-old confidence tricks, it is the sheer scale of the scams that is new.

Computers and telephony have these advantages for scammers:

- They provide anonymity. You have no idea who is contacting you. Whoever is on the telephone or sending out emails can take on any persona to suit the scam.

- People can't get back at the scammers. You don't know who they are and they can block return calls so they don't have to suffer your anger. They can just disappear.

- Technology is cheap. Email accounts are available free. Landlines can be rented with a package that allows free calls to other landlines within the country. Mobile phone packages include a large number of free calls per month plus unlimited texts.

- Technology is fast and automatic. Scammers can generate emails rapidly or have a computer constantly dialling telephone numbers so there is always a new victim waiting on the line when they finish the previous call.

- Scammers can get victims to work for them by gaining access to the email addresses on other people's computers. Thus the number of people who can be contacted multiplies.

- Victims can often be persuaded to damage their own computer software, which means scammers can make money by offering to put right the very fault that they created.

- Most computer users have only basic knowledge of the machine they are using, so they can easily be fooled with technical jargon.

- Once a potential victim replies to an email the scammer knows that the account is active.

- Loads of personal information is easily available on the internet, much of it provided by the potential victims themselves on social media.

- Although cybercrime has become increasingly sophisticated, criminals require only limited technical knowledge to operate lucrative scams.

Anything goes

Hackers will steal anything of value. Nothing is sacred. For example, one gang hacked into British Airways' Executive Club scheme and stole points. One member reported that his account had been used by someone else to book a hotel room in Spain, while others reported that their list of transactions showed 'ex-gratia' deductions that had wiped out their entire credit.

Another member found that his mobile phone number had been changed to a Russian one. Luckily he managed to change it back before his air miles could be used.

The weakest link

The problem for companies holding customer information online is that if they warn customers it brings bad publicity, but if they keep quiet the consequences can be far worse.

However security conscious a company is, employees are the weakest link. Opening an email or clicking on a link can seem quite innocuous and employees are likely to receive different files from a wider range of sources than they would on their own computer at home.

Many businesses, including banks, are reluctant to report online crimes, partly because they fear the publicity will hurt them commercially and partly because they feel there is little chance that the perpetrators will be caught.

Instead, the businesses absorb the cost of the scam and either the shareholders or the customers effectively pick up the bill.

Low-risk, high-reward crime

There are in effect often no sanctions against hi-tech scammers. Many work from abroad, out of reach of the regulators and law enforcement agencies that try to protect the victims. Telephone calls that purport to come from within this country can in fact originate abroad and be rerouted domestically.

Thus, for one reason or another, cyber crime has become a lucrative, low-risk form of theft.

It is impossible to calculate the true scale of cybercrime because no one knows how much goes unreported. Figures from the City of London Police, which leads police operations in the UK in investigating fraud and prosecuting the perpetrators, suggest that 85% of cybercrime goes unreported. If that is so, then 70% of all fraud is now carried out on the internet.

Email scammers have access to lists of email addresses that can be bought cheaply. They can contact millions of internet subscribers in a second. Some addresses may be incorrect or dormant but it doesn't matter. The scammer is into high volume. If only a tiny fraction of 1% of people approached actually bite, the scammer can make a good living. Each victim is likely to produce a high return.

There is no escape

Potential victims can innocently identify themselves to scammers. Unsubscribing from a mailing list may not put an end to the junk emails. On the contrary, it confirms to the scammers that this is a genuine, active email address. It is better to put up with the junk email and hope it dwindles when the scammers get no response, or use the 'junk' or 'mark as spam' function provided within your email account.

Similarly, pressing a button on your telephone when prompted to do so by an automated call tells the scammer that yours is a real number in current use.

You can take evasive action but the effect is likely to be limited and is no substitute for being constantly on your guard. For example, while it is possible to register with the telecoms regulator Ofcom to have genuine UK sales calls blocked, scammers ignore the rules. Don't hope for any help from the authorities in the countries where the phone scammers are based. They naturally flourish in countries where regulation is limited and the authorities are unlikely to offer much cooperation with police enquiries.

Spoofing

Many modern handsets have Caller ID, which shows the caller's number on screen. The idea is that you can decline to answer calls from numbers you don't recognise.

However, the battle between law enforcers and hi-tech scammers is rather like vaccines and bacteria. The baddies are always finding new ways to thrive. There have been growing instances of nuisance callers and criminals deliberately changing the Caller ID, which is a practice known as 'spoofing'.

Calls with spoofed numbers can and do come from all over the world and account for a significant and growing proportion of nuisance calls.

Sometimes there's a good reason for a caller to modify the Caller ID, for example to provide a freephone number that you can call back.

Spoofing callers deliberately change the telephone number and/or name relayed as the Caller ID information either to hide their identity or to mimic the number of a real company or person. Scammers who want to steal sensitive information such as your bank account or login details sometimes use spoofing to pretend they're calling from your bank or credit card company.

The rule is that you should not rely entirely on Caller ID as a guarantee of the caller's identification.

Postal addresses

Some overseas scammers use a UK address. If you are able to visit it you will find that it is merely a rented postal address where one person collects mail for a range of businesses.

The office manager will genuinely have no idea where the scammer is really operating from. The scammer will just pop in from time to time to pick up any mail.

Working in teams

Scammers often work in teams or at least in pairs. If you speak to more than one person in the course of the scam it helps to build the impression that it is a bona fide office at a genuine company contacting you.

In some scams an appointment is made for a 'senior adviser' to call back. This flatters you into thinking you are getting special treatment. You certainly are, but not in the way you hope.

This is the signal for you to be offered expensive investments with the promise of high rates of return. They may be in schemes such as trading in options of foreign exchange, where you have heard that big money is made in the blink of an eye but you don't quite understand how.

The 'senior adviser' is persistent and will make you feel foolish for not understanding the opportunity or if you ask for further explanation.

The information age

Scammers can be very good at finding out about the people they target. Information about all of us is out there on the internet, often provided by ourselves on social media. For example, they are able to promise those with specific religious or community interests that some investments and/or profits will be channelled into charities or worthy causes as a way to reel in their victims.

How we can beat the scammers

There are several simple measures you can take to avoid falling into modern-day traps:

1. Never open emails from unknown senders and in particular never open attachments or click on any links they contain. Delete them from your inbox and empty the email trash folder.

2. Even if you know the sender, be careful of opening attachments or clicking on links in suspicious or strange looking emails. The sender's email address book may have been hijacked.

3. Do not open an email unless you are sure you know the sender or it is an email you were expecting.

4. Do not open emails that come from peculiar addresses that contain loads of random letters that do not spell words or names.

5. Do not open emails that promise you services or benefits that you have not requested.

6. If your email provider offers you the option of reporting emails as spam or junk then make full use of this facility. It is far easier to empty the spam folder en masse rather than delete each item individually.

7. Provide your contact details only to people you trust. This is far from being full protection against scammers but it helps

to narrow down the scope for scammers to come across your email by chance.

8. Set-up a separate email address for use on public sites such as social media.

Maintaining up-to-date security software on your computer is a sensible precaution but do not assume you are completely safe. Hackers are always trying to devise new malware and the good guys are left reacting to each new attack. It doesn't help that Microsoft withdraws security support from older but still widely used Windows operating systems.

The first internet scam to gain widespread recognition was phishing, so let's look at that phenomenon first.

CHAPTER 17.
The Phishing Scam

PHISHING IS THE TERM GIVEN TO THE PRACTICE OF SENDING an email that purports to come from a bank or some other reputable organisation in an attempt to lure recipients into revealing their personal information, such as credit card numbers, internet passwords or bank details.

The one thing you can say in its favour is that it brought the dangers of doing business electronically in the modern age to the attention of anyone who was prepared to take notice. Sadly, a lot of people seem to bury their heads in the sand and the scammers continue to thrive.

Phishing is so popular among scammers that it has become part of everyday life. Few days will pass without you being on the receiving end of a phishing attempt.

The messages have got more sophisticated over time but the original scam was to ask you to click on reply and confirm your login and password, perhaps as a routine check or because someone had tried to take over your account and you needed to reestablish that it was yours.

The scammer then logged into your account, changed the password and took over the account. In the meantime you were blocked out and confused because you did not understand why you could no longer log in. It took time for victims to realise what had happened and get it sorted.

Early efforts were pretty crude but because the scam was not well known it worked like a charm. Victims unwittingly handed over the keys to their accounts. When they next tried to log in they found someone else was in control.

Scammers became more sophisticated

Before the scam became widely recognised, banks and other organisations could be slow to react, not believing that accounts had been compromised. Despite the considerable publicity that has been given to this scam, people still fall for it.

This is partly because scammers have become more sophisticated. Spelling and grammatical errors that were a big giveaway in the early days have been ironed out and designs have been improved so that emails look as if they really do come from organisation they purport to. Logos are copied carefully to closely resemble the real thing.

More accomplished phishers have also learnt to avoid using obviously false email addresses by registering addresses that are more closely aligned to the organisation they pretend to represent. The following is an example.

We observed multiple login attempts

From: Barclays Bank (Barclays@email.barclays.co.uk)
Dear Customer,

We recently have determined that different computers have logged in your Barclays account, and multiple password failures were present before the logons.

Do not ignore this message is four your security.

For your security we have temporary suspended your account. Please download the document attached to this email and fill carefully.

If you do not restore your account within 24 hours, we will be forced to suspend your account indefinitely, as it may have been used for fraudulent purposes.

We apologize for any inconvenience.

Some work is still required on polishing up the English but this attempt to panic the recipient may still be effective. Downloading and filling in the form will hand your details to the scammer.

A similar fate awaits anyone who ignores the peculiar email address and equally peculiar English on this message that certainly did not come from PayPal.

PayPal: Account Access Limited

Paypal (kuljetusnupponen@kolumbus.fi)

Dear Paypal User,

Your Paypal account has been become limited. to restore full access to your account follow the instruction on the attached PDF file.

Yours sincerely,

PayPal

Why it is called phishing

Phishing got its name from the similarity to an angler trying to catch fish. You are the fish and you are offered bait. It is popular because people seem to readily fall for it, despite the fact that most phishing scams are quite obvious.

Its other attraction for scammers is that it is fast and cheap so messages can be scattered on the water like breadcrumbs. It just takes a few victims to bite to make it worthwhile.

If you learn to recognise the types of bait floating around you can avoid the nasty hook. They are:

1. **You need to act fast**. You are told you will suffer some dire consequence such as an account being terminated if you do not quickly follow the instructions in the message.

2. **Wouldn't you like to know?** There is some interesting information available but the message is rather vague on what precisely it is.

3. **Hello, old friend**. The message seems to come from someone you know or you are told that an important message is waiting for you from a friend, although it may not be clear who the message is from.

Phishers tend to select individual banks one by one as the supposed source of the email and bombard as many email addresses as possible. Only a fraction of recipients will actually have an account at that bank and only a fraction of those will fall for the trick, but it only needs a tiny number to be deceived to make it worthwhile.

The scammers then try another bank to rake in a fresh load of victims. If you receive a phishing email and respond to say you don't use the bank in question, you have alerted the scammers to the fact that your email address is active and you have taken the email seriously. You have also narrowed down your choice of bank and will be bombarded with similar emails purporting to come from other banks until the scammer gets the right one.

Despite repeated warnings from banks that they never email you to ask for your password, PIN or account number, the phishing scam reappears after a suitable gap to allow memories to fade. Nor do frequent reports in the press appear to discourage victims from succumbing.

Any account will do

It is not only bank accounts that are at risk. Any online account that stores information about you – particularly your bank or card details – can be targeted. The scammer persuades you to release your account name and password, then they log in as you and order goods to be delivered to them at your expense.

Online auction site eBay says it has reduced incidents where scammers take over accounts as its detection systems usually identify these attempts before any harm is done and such instances are now extremely rare. Where an account is hijacked, eBay says it quickly regains control of the account.

It's up to you

However, you should not rely on eBay or any other company to rescue you from your own carelessness. Scammers may still get control of your account and order goods, or 'sell' nonexistent goods and divert the money away from your PayPal account and into theirs.

One eBay account holder received notification from eBay that, following his request, it had changed the password on his account. He had made no such request. Then eBay notified him of two listings of mechanical road rollers that had been put up for sale on his account.

One buyer actually paid £2,300 for one of the road rollers. The prompt action of the account holder meant that the money was returned. The account holder very sensibly suspended his PayPal account to stop buyers putting money in for non-existent goods and the scammer from taking money out.

When this sort of thing happens you can find yourself spending a lot of time and effort sorting out the mess. Better not to fall for it in the first place. NEVER reveal your password for any account of any description in response to an email or a telephone call.

One other point worth noting is that you could find yourself buying from someone whose account has been hijacked. There is no way of knowing for sure but warning bells should ring if a seller pushes for speedy completion of the transaction and requests quick payment.

How we can beat the scammers

These scams often rely on arousing your curiosity. You should be more suspicious if you want to avoid getting hooked.

Check it out

If you know where the message has come from, ask the sender if the message is genuine.

DO NOT do this by hitting reply. If it's a scam, you may be going back to the scammer who will, naturally, assure you it is bona fide.

Send a separate email or better still phone the sender. If a friend's email has been hacked they will want to be warned.

Ignore links in the email

DO NOT check the authenticity of the message by clicking on any link in the email that purports to give further information. This is what the scammer wants you to do.

Instead, close the message and search for the sender or the subject matter through your own search engine. You may find that other people have reported the message as a scam or are questioning its authenticity, in which case you can assume that it is not genuine.

If the message gives the name of a company, find and access that company's website separately to see if it is genuine. Then type in any code given in the message in the appropriate box or enter the subject matter into the site's search facility. If the contact is genuine, you will find out what the message is all about.

Ignore attachments

This is where any malware will lie. Open it and you are doomed. Malware ranges from destroying your computer's operating system to stealing your financial details, including passwords. Any type of attachment can be infected, including Microsoft Word documents and PDFs.

If you were not expecting the file, do not open it even if it appears to have come from a friend.

Maintain security

At the very least, set your computer or other device to automatically download any available security updates. Extra anti-virus software to scan files and attachments for malware can be bought or downloaded free on the internet. The software may even be able to check if links in emails are safe.

This may save you from your own foolishness but do not relax. An attachment is not guaranteed to be just because it has slipped though the net. Scammers are always devising new malware to try to get one step ahead, so you still need to be careful.

Visit your bank's website

Many large companies, particularly banks, have information on their websites explaining how to stay safe from phishing, along with ways to report phishing cases to them. They may also give examples of recent scams that are circulating.

Report any attacks

Publicising any phishing attempts, whether you fell for them or not, adds to the general good. Remember that if people stopped falling for phishing scams there would be fewer of them about.

Report the scam to whoever's name was taken in vain, whether it was a private email address or a company. Spread the word by social media.

Out of phishing came vishing, where a human voice replaces the impersonal email. We'll look at this in the next chapter.

CHAPTER 18.
The Vishing Scam

THE VISHING SCAM IS A MORE SOPHISTICATED VARIANT OF the phishing scam. It works in the same way but instead of contacting you online the fraudster calls you on the phone. V in vishing stands for voice.

There are several varieties of vishing scams and the message keeps changing as scams are publicised and people become more wary. You may be asked to:

- Give details of your bank account, particularly answers to security questions.

- Transfer money into another account.

- Hand over your credit and debit card details.

Your account is being raided

Typically, the fraudster phones you claiming to be from your bank. He will give a fictitious but plausible name and say he is ringing from the bank's fraud department.

He convinces you that someone is trying to move money fraudulently out of your account at that very moment. You need to transfer the money yourself, using telephone or internet banking, to prevent the theft. The scammer gives you a sort code and account number to transfer the money to.

The account is said to be in your name and using a different bank branch is essential to put the money beyond the reach of the people trying to raid your account.

Why the scam works

The essence of the scam is to convince you of the urgency of taking action immediately. You are panicked into doing as the scammer says so you do not have time to think things through.

What makes this scam particularly effective is that the fraudster often uses computer software to alter the number he appears to be calling from. If you have Caller ID then it may show the call as coming from your bank's fraud department – a number you can easily check on your bank statement.

Even more frightening is that several people who have been taken in say that the caller had details of their bank balance and the type of accounts they had, such as current, savings and ISAs.

In some cases victims have contacted their bank's fraud department before transferring the money and have been reassured that the transfer sounds legitimate because fraud departments do often contact account holders to query suspicious activity, such as uncharacteristic spending patterns involving large amounts of money. So if someone really were trying to empty your account it is quite likely that the fraud department would be in touch.

If you are calling your bank's fraud department in a case like this, ask them to check carefully to see if there is any note on file to suggest your account is currently under investigation.

Of course, the scammer is not your bank's fraud department. Under the scam, you are moving the money into an account set up by the scammer, possibly an account that has been opened some time earlier and operated as a normal account to avert suspicion. The money will then be transferred onwards, probably abroad to put it out of reach, and the account you transferred the money to will be closed.

Who pays?

Banks are very reluctant to reimburse any money lost in this way, since it is you, not the bank, that fell for the scam. You authorised the transfer of the money.

If you contacted your bank before making the transfer and show that the bank led you to believe that the call was genuine, you are far more likely to get your money refunded. After all, the bank should have checked its own computer records and to see that no one from its fraud department had contacted you.

Also, if you fall for this scam but realise you have been conned, then alerting your bank as quickly as possible may limit the amount that is stolen and even mean that cash already transferred can be recovered before the scammer moves it out of reach.

The fatal flaw

Had you not been panicked into doing what the fraudster told you to do and had time to stop and think, you might well have seen the flaw in this scam.

If someone really is trying to steal money out of your account, why can't the bank simply block the transfer? If the call really is from your bank, you can simply say that you have not authorised the transaction and the bank will stop it.

After all, this is what happens when the bank rings you to say that a suspicious item has come through on your credit card. You tell the bank it is not genuine and they block the payment.

If the bank did allow the unauthorised transfer of money out of your account then the bank, not you, would be responsible and it would have to reimburse you.

The question of who is to blame and who should bear the loss is, admittedly, a contentious one. Aggrieved account holders feel, understandably, that they thought they were acting on the bank's instructions and therefore they are innocent victims. This is particularly so when the scammer has details of their accounts.

Banks argue that if you authorise the transfer then it is your fault. You, not the bank, are the victim, they argue. Banks are often castigated for holding up and querying authorised payments that may be urgent, yet they are accused of not blocking fraudulent transfers.

The bank may also feel that account holders who are reimbursed will not be encouraged to take greater care if they are subsequently approached by another scammer in the future.

An inspector calls

In another variation of the vishing scam, you receive a telephone call at home, purporting to come from your bank or from the police. They suspect that your card has been cloned and they will name a couple of shops some distance from your home that, they hope, you have not visited. In any case, you can hardly be at home and have been in the shops just a few minutes earlier so they are on pretty safe ground.

Having got you to panic, the scammer will do everything possible to set your mind at rest. The fake card has been stopped, the false transactions have been reversed so there is no financial loss to you. The culprits have been detained so they can do no further harm. Your card has been frozen, which may be a little inconvenient, but your bank will issue a replacement within a few days.

The difficulty of dealing with this kind of scam is that it could be a genuine call from your bank's fraud department. In that case you need to be fully cooperative and nip the problem in the bud.

As further reassurance, the scammer will encourage you to put the phone down and ring up your bank's fraud department. He will tell you his name, which will be fictitious, and tell you to ask for him when you ring back.

The line stays open

The scammer does not put down the phone, though. He will keep the line open, so when you pick up the receiver you are still connected to him. Vishing scammers work in teams and a different voice will be on the line when you think you have rung back, as would quite likely happen if you really were through to the fraud department. You are then transferred to the original scammer.

To create a greater sense of panic, some scammers claim to be from the police rather than the bank. Such is the persuasive power of these people, they have actually convinced victims that it is possible to dial 999 and ask to be put through to the specific police officer supposedly handling your case.

This is simply not possible. If you dial 999 and ask for police you will be put through to a control room, not an individual officer.

The butler wait

The reason for the delay in the line being cut off lies in a curious quirk of British history. Since the inception of the telephone system it has been the case in the UK that if the caller puts the phone down, the call is disconnected immediately, but if the recipient puts the phone down the line stays open.

The delay is known in the telecoms industry as the Butler Wait. It takes one back to the more leisurely days of the popular television programme *Downton Abbey*.

Since in the past only the rich could afford telephones, and they also had butlers, it was the norm for the butler to answer the phone in his den and inquire for which member of the household the call was intended.

He would then put the receiver down and toddle off to find the relevant person, who would take the call in the hall safe in the knowledge that the caller was still on the line and no one was listening in below stairs. Thus the line had to be kept open for a couple of minutes.

Ringing back

So when you call back, try to use another phone such as your mobile or a neighbour's phone to check with your bank.

If you have to use the same phone line, listen carefully to whether there is a dialling tone. When the line has been kept open there usually will not be one, although scammers have become alert to this flaw in their operation. Some play a fake dial tone down the line when you think you are redialling.

The line may stay open for two minutes before it is cut off automatically, so wait for at least three minutes.

BT is working on changes to its equipment that will cut calls off more quickly when one end rings off, but do not rely on this and remember that many other telecoms providers use BT exchanges and are similarly affected. Sky and TalkTalk have improved their system to cut off calls when one party hangs up.

Catching out the scammers

Telephone scammers often rely heavily on you providing them with information, usually by getting you to answer security questions. This can be convincing because your bank really would want to be sure that it was talking to the account holder.

You can turn this to your advantage. Did the caller say which bank he was calling from? If he said "Your bank" or "The Bank" he doesn't know which bank to say.

Suppose you have an account with NatWest. Ask the caller: "Are you from Barclays or Lloyds?" If the caller selects a bank that you have no dealings with then you are quite sure from the start that the call is not genuine.

It is possible that the caller does know which bank you are with. After all, every time you issue a cheque you hand over your name, your bank's name, which branch you use and your account number.

Deliberately get one of the security questions wrong, such as giving a false name for your mother's maiden name or the wrong year of your birth. The scammer is unlikely to have these details, which is why he is asking you for them. If the incorrect answer goes unchallenged, you are dealing with a scammer.

Even if the caller spots your traps, indicating that it really might be the bank, proceed with caution. Your date of birth and your mother's maiden name can be found by a well-prepared scammer. Above all else, do not reveal:

- Any password you use.

- Your PIN.

  You bank will NEVER ask for these.

The barbarian at the gate

Having extracted from you sufficient information to use your card, all the scammer needs is the card itself.

You are told that the bank/police need your genuine card so that it can be compared with the cloned version.

A motorcyclist will be despatched to your house forthwith – note that once again time is of the essence, otherwise you may smell a rat. You are to hand over the card in a sealed envelope to the courier, who is not allowed to speak to you.

As he will be wearing a motorcycle helmet, you will not see his face or hear his voice so you cannot identify him in the unlikely event that he is subsequently apprehended.

Don't hand over your card

If you get conned into parting with your details – scammers can be very persuasive – you have one last line of defence: Do NOT hand over any credit or debit cards to a courier sent to your door.

Neither your bank nor the police will ever ask you to do this. The card is absolutely useless to them. Nothing on it can possibly shed any light on how, when or by whom the card was cloned. Nor can it tell them where a cloned card was used.

I read in the newspapers of one victim who thought he had covered himself by snipping the card in two before handing it over, but the scammers still found a way to use the card.

Bad service

You should assume that any call purporting to be from a service provider, such as mobile phone or utility company, is a scam if the caller:

- Quotes your bank account number. Far from this being proof that the call is genuine, it indicates that the scammer has hacked into your service provider's computer and stolen your personal details.

- Asks you to provide bank details unless you have already given specific permission to the service provider to ask for this information.

- Asks you to download software onto your computer.

- Asks you to provide your full password.

How we can beat the scammers

- Never give your PIN or passwords to a caller.

- Never hand your card to anyone except a member of staff in a branch of your bank.

- Ring your bank to check if the call was genuine, preferably from a different phone to the one you were called on. If that is not possible then allow a delay of at least three minutes.

Apart from sending a motorcycle courier round to your home, there are many ways in which scammers can gain access to your plastic, including more subtle ways of persuading you to hand your card over, as we shall see in the next chapter.

CHAPTER 19.
Card Machine Scams

I T MAY SEEM UNSOPHISTICATED BY MODERN STANDARDS, AND each individual haul is quite small, but robbing people immediately after they have used a cash point has some big advantages:

- The scammer knows the victim has money
- He gets cash in hand
- There is no paper or electronic trail that leads back to him

Simply grabbing the money and legging it is just plain theft, but scammers look for ways of getting hold of the card and using it themselves.

Some culprits have taken to hiding cameras above the keyboard to record PINs. There have been cases of an iPod being taped to the machine for this purpose.

The advent of 3D printers has allowed scammers to manufacture fake keypads or even a whole cash machine front.

Shoulder surfing

The most basic scam is when someone looks over your shoulder to see you type in your PIN, then steals your card and uses it to withdraw cash in another machine or to pay for goods.

Stealing the card involves distracting the victim, so scammers tend to pick on the elderly, those who look preoccupied or someone laden with shopping.

One method is to drop a credit card on the floor then ask the person leaving the ATM if they have dropped it. It throws victims off guard because they feel as if they are being helpful.

Another distraction is to offer to help the victim use the machine, often after jamming the machine's card slot to stop it accepting cards. Or they may cancel the transaction without the victim realising then slip the card into their pocket.

Skimming

Once the scammer has the card, it is inserted into a device – a skimmer – that records electronic details from the magnetic strip. The details can be recovered and used by the scammer or they may be relayed automatically through mobile phone technology to an accomplice.

The electronic data is used to clone the card. Often the perpetrator will have looked over the cardholder's shoulder to memorise the PIN or a hidden camera will record which numbers the cardholder pressed.

The beauty of this scam, from the fraudster's point of view, is that the cardholder is unaware that the card has been skimmed. Cash is dispensed and the card is returned as in a normal transaction.

Lebanese loop

Another method also involves inserting a device into the ATM but this time the card is retained in the machine by a metal or plastic strip or sleeve looped inside the card slot. Again, there may be a hidden camera to record the PIN as it is entered.

In some cases the cash is also retained in the machine until the scammers come along and release it.

Scammers hope the victim will assume the machine has retained the card and they will be able to get it from inside the branch. This scam is often used when the bank is closed so that the victim will give up and walk away, intending to come back when the branch is open.

The card machine scam

Our credit and debit cards are at their most vulnerable when they are out of our hands. You should never let yours be any further out of sight than necessary.

Hard-learnt lessons are often forgotten over time, which is why effective scams often lie dormant for a while before bouncing back.

In the early days of credit cards, waiters used to take the card away from the diner and process it behind a counter. The ensuing publicity about cards being processed twice or cloned encouraged diners to insist on accompanying the waiter to the card machine so that the card was never out of sight. Subsequently banks introduced card machines that can be brought to the table.

Some establishments still insist on keeping a card behind the bar so that a night's food and drinks can be paid for in one go rather than round by round. The reputation of a respectable establishment may put cardholders off guard.

This is, however, an open invitation for bar staff to add bogus drinks or mix up your tally with someone else's, or to steal your card details.

Do not assume that if the establishment is highly respectable everything will automatically be fine – be on your guard if you are asked to hand over your card. Review all receipts carefully and check your card bill or bank statement as soon as you can to ensure you have only paid for what you ordered.

How we can beat the scammers

There are things you can do to cut down the risk of being the next victim:

- If anything about a cash machine looks at all suspicious, don't use it. In particular, check if anything on the front of the machine looks unusual.

- When the bank is open, use a machine inside the building if possible rather than one outside that is more open to sabotage.

- Keep both hands spread out above the keypad to obscure the view as you enter your PIN.

- Choose cash machines in well-lit areas and look round before using one. Don't be afraid to let anyone in the vicinity of the machine know that you have seen them.

- Don't use the machine if someone is standing right behind you and crowding you.

- Ignore anyone who tries to talk to you while you are using the machine.

- Put your card and cash away quickly, preferably in an inside pocket.

- Whether or not you eventually extract your card, report any incident to the card issuer immediately. Don't just walk away.

- Do not let your card out of sight.

- If you have the slightest suspicion that your card has been stolen or cloned, tell your bank immediately so the card can be cancelled. The inconvenience of being without a card for a few days until a new one arrives is nothing compared to having a thief run up debts at your expense.

The expanding use of debit and credit cards has taught bank account holders the convenience of not having to carry large amounts of cash around. It is a natural progression to move onto online banking, not only for account holders but also for scammers. We move on to look at online banking scams next.

CHAPTER 20.
Online Banking Scams

A S MORE PEOPLE MAKE USE OF ONLINE BANKING, associated fraud inevitably increases. Losses from online banking fraud rose by 48% to £60 million in 2014, according to Financial Fraud Action UK, an organisation set up by the financial services industry to coordinate activity on fraud prevention and detection.

The rise is due to increased use of computer malware and con-artists tricking consumers out of personal details.

It could have been worse. Financial Fraud Action called the aggregate amount stolen "relatively modest", considering that more than half of UK adults use online banking.

The stolen phone line

Conmen will steal just about anything – even your telephone line. In a highly sophisticated type of banking fraud they divert calls from the victim's phone line, then pretend to be the customer when the bank rings up to query a payment set up by the criminals.

Criminals call the victim's telephone company and arrange for calls to be redirected. This does not arouse the phone company's suspicion as most landline providers have a call divert service so that incoming calls go automatically to another landline or mobile number. This is useful for customers who want to stay in contact when they are away from home.

It is true that the scammer needs personal details to take over the line, but a lot of personal information is freely available and conmen are particularly adept at finding it. Most people's telephone numbers are included in directories and even if you are ex-directory you should not assume you are safe from this scam.

When the scammers put through a fraudulent payment into their own account and the bank rings to query it, the call is diverted to the scammer. The bank thinks it is talking to the real account holder and accepts the scammer's assurance that the transaction is genuine.

Since the account holder is still able to make outgoing calls, it may take time for him or her to realise that there is something wrong with the phone and that no calls are coming in.

Banks are attempting to counteract this fraud by installing software that tells them when a call has been diverted. This alerts the bank to the possibility that a customer's phone has been hijacked and that the unusual payment may well be a scam. It is part of the constant battle between scammers and financial institutions to stay ahead of each other.

The banks have a great incentive to put a stop to this scam. As they, rather than the account holders, are the ones being duped, they have an obligation to reimburse any money that is stolen.

Ever on a Friday

While scammers operate round the clock, each and every day, it seems that Friday is when we are most vulnerable to online banking fraud. The thinking is that money withdrawn on Friday may not be spotted until Monday, when it will be too late to recover the loss.

Some financial institutions do not have staff on duty over the weekend, so even if you want to raise a query you may not be able to do so.

More people book trips online these days rather than going to a high street travel agent. Thus any fraudster who hacks into your email account knows exactly when you are going to be away. That provides a longer window of time to make any illegal transfer of cash from the victim's account to the scammer's and extends the time before the theft is discovered.

Computer hackers can often glean enough information to access your accounts with your bank or investment provider. Most people use an easy to remember password such as a child's name. Date of birth is generally used as a security check, but we have to give this so often on forms that the hacker can easily find this somewhere on your computer.

If you have used your computer for any kind of financial transaction, to make purchases from online retailers or paid utility and tax bills online, you are likely to have left a trail of clues.

The scammer then gains access to your account and changes the password to shut you out. If an account at an investment provider is the target, he then changes the nominated bank account into which any outward payments are made. He can divert money from your account into his and possibly sell some of your assets and take the proceeds.

Most large banks will contact a customer to verify changes to online banking details but not all do and investment providers are less likely to do so.

While banks usually have a fraud department line open 24/7, not all do and investment providers, through which you channel savings into funds and ISAs, may not have a helpline or customer service line available at weekends.

These are particular targets for fraudsters, who use Faster Payments, an electronic transfer system that allows money to be moved within minutes. It is used legitimately by companies needing to make payments quickly and also by many people purchasing homes for buy to let, so this method of money transfer does not in itself throw up alarm signals.

One-time passcodes

Banks sometimes provide, via a text message, a 'one-time passcode' to be used for a specific telephone banking transfer.

Scammers may ring you and ask for this code, claiming that they need to prevent a fraudulent transfer of funds out of your account. Instead, they use the passcode to pass the money to their own account. You should never divulge a one-time passcode any more than you should tell a third party any other code or password.

The bank is providing this code to you. Why on earth would it ask you to give the code to its fraud department? Anyone who asks you to hand over your passcode is a scammer. There are no exceptions.

Money mules

One potential difficulty for scammers is that when they set up bank accounts to receive their ill-gotten gains they are asked to provide evidence of their name and address, including photographic ID, and a utility bill. This means that they are at risk of being traced when they commit a fraud.

Despite the supposedly stringent tests that sometimes cause great inconvenience to genuine customers apply for a new account, scammers seem to be able to get around the barriers with false ID.

If they are unable to set-up their own account, some use 'money mules'. The fraudster offers a genuine bank account holder, or someone willing to set up an account, a fee in return for agreeing to accept a payment and pass the cash on to another account held by the scammer. This at least puts the scammer one step away from the long arm of the law.

Money mules are typically students, job seekers or recent immigrants – people who are likely to be hard up and willing to earn a bit of pocket money with no questions asked.

Anyone who allows their account to be used in this way faces up to ten years in jail. Ignorance is no defence. Ask yourself: do you really think that such an arrangement could possibly be legitimate? Why doesn't the person who has approached you have an account, or set one up?

As with so many scams, just a moment's quiet reflection will allow you to smell a rat.

The bogus solicitor

Scammers are always looking for new angles on old scams. Having successfully defrauded large numbers of victims by posing as bank officials and then police officers, they have moved on to posing as solicitors. This is a particularly useful tactic when it comes to online banking.

The Solicitors Regulation Authority (SRA), which regulates solicitors in England and Wales, has expressed growing concerns about fraudsters impersonating law firms and is issuing an increasing number of alerts on its website, mainly involving emails but also including letters and phone calls. Scammers also use fake websites that purport to belong to solicitors.

The SRA says it recorded 701 reports about bogus law firms in 2014, up from 312 in 2012. The Law Society of Scotland has also said that the number of fake firms is on the rise.

Property sales

People buying property, and those advising them, are particularly good targets for scammers posing as solicitors because of the large sums of money involved. Potential hauls run into thousands, even hundreds of thousands, of pounds.

Some reported cases have involved bogus solicitors using the name of a genuine law firm when pretending to be acting for the vendor of a property. The purchaser's conveyancer hands over cash to complete the sale, whereupon the 'solicitor' disappears.

In such cases the genuine law firm is completely unaware it is being used in a scam and is, in a way, also a victim because its good name is tarnished.

In other cases fraudsters send emails that appear to be from the victims' solicitors. The house purchaser is directed to transfer money to fake accounts. Often the victim is only too pleased to oblige, as this is taken as a sign that all is going well and completion is imminent.

The fraudster may also send emails to the solicitor, pretending to be the client, to prevent the fraud being detected before the funds are moved into the fraudster's account and then abroad out of reach.

By the time the fraud is detected, it may be too late to recover the money. Banks may refuse to issue refunds because the transfers have been authorised by the customers.

The dangers of using public Wi-Fi

The *Sunday Times* reported that a woman from southeast London was completing on a flat she had bought at auction. As she would be on holiday when the final payment was to be made, she arranged for her bank to pay the £137,000 in her absence.

The day before the money was due, she emailed her solicitors using the Wi-Fi service in the hotel to ask for the details of the bank account she should transfer the money into. Later that day she checked her emails and found a genuine one from the solicitors giving the correct bank and account number.

However, a second email, from scammers who had intercepted the messages, said that the solicitors were having account issues and that the money should be sent to a different bank. Details of the sort code and account number were supplied.

The woman rang her bank and arranged for payment to be made to the second, bogus account. She emailed her solicitors to say that the transfer had been made and asking for confirmation that completion on the purchase had taken place.

Intercepting emails

The fraudsters intercepted her email and also those from her solicitor saying the money had not been received. Further emails sent over the following two days were also intercepted and deleted. Instead, the fraudsters sent reassuring emails in both directions.

The scammers told the solicitors that the bank had used BACS, a slower method of transferring funds, rather than the faster Chaps system, which accounted for the delay. They told the flat buyer that the money had been received and the deal had completed.

The three-day leeway before the buyer returned home to discover the awful truth gave the scammers enough time to transfer the money abroad and disappear. By the time the scammers' account had been blocked, only £1,000 remained in it.

Wi-Fi connections available to the general public such as those at hotels and airports will usually put up a message on screen advising you that the system is not secure. You have been warned.

If you must make a transaction using a public connection, ring the recipient separately to ascertain that any messages you receive are genuine. Do not type in card numbers or bank account details. Make any payments before you go on holiday if possible. It is better to lose the use of the money for a few days than to lose the money altogether.

How we can beat the scammers

- Maintain firewalls and security on your computer.
- Avoid using public networks.
- If you have the tiniest suspicion that something is wrong, do not go ahead with a transaction.

Apart from hacking into your bank account, scammers can do a lot of other damage by gaining access to the wealth of information stored in your computer. We move on to look at this next.

CHAPTER 21.
Computer Scams

I F YOU ARE LUCKY, A COMPUTER SCAM WILL SIMPLY INVOLVE
inflicting damage on your computer. You end up paying
£40 (at least) for your friendly neighbourhood problem fixer
to run an anti-malware program on your machine and you
continue a little wiser and a little poorer.

Some hackers simply regard messing up your computer as
a bit of harmless fun, rather in the way that a yob might leave
a breeze block underneath a cardboard box in the middle of
the road to watch an unsuspecting motorist smash up the car's
sump.

Far more likely, however, is that a computer hacker has
something much more malevolent in mind: stealing personal
information stored in your computer, especially details of bank
and other financial accounts along with PINs and passwords.

Searching for the bug

Although it is not a financial scam as such, one of the earliest and most persistent hoaxes is worth relaying as there are lessons to be learnt from it.

It originated in Brazil and began to circulate via email in Portuguese before being translated into various languages because so many people fell for it. You were encouraged to look for a bug which, the email claimed, might be lying dormant within your computer's operating system waiting to spring suddenly into life, at which point it would erase everything on your hard drive.

The warning email gave detailed instructions on how to check whether the 'bug' was in your computer and how to remove it. The great success of this hoax was that everybody who fell for it did indeed find the 'bug' present. That was because it was not a bug but an essential part of every computer's operating system.

Victims hastened to pass the message on to all their friends. Thus they perpetuated the hoax, which required no further effort on the part of the hoaxers.

This fairly harmless prank, which brought no benefit to the hoaxers and merely inconvenienced the victims, demonstrated how easy it is to deceive people with limited knowledge of how computers operate and opened the door to more sophisticated scams. It showed how well-meaning victims can be tricked into spreading the word.

The Microsoft imposter

Fraudulent phone calls from people claiming to be computer experts are on the rise. The aim is either to get you to pay to correct non-existent faults on your computer or to gain access to your bank or credit card details.

The caller claims to be from a company with Microsoft in its title, such as Microsoft Service Company. In fact neither he, nor his company if it really exists, has anything to do with Microsoft. If you persist with a demand for a yes/no answer to the question "Are you employed by Microsoft?" you may actually extract an admission that he is not.

The scammer will claim that emails you have sent indicate that there is a virus in your computer. This is absolute tosh. There is no way that the caller can know whether your computer is infected or not. However, the caller is relying on the fact that most people are not computer-savvy and they are terrified of losing all the data on their machine.

The scammer will ask you to run a specific program on your computer and will then ask you or tell you what is showing on the screen. This may in fact be an indication that the program is running correctly.

The scammer will claim falsely that your screen is indicating that there is indeed a virus installed. It's a very clever and convincing hoax because what is on your screen is totally unfamiliar to you, although it would be instantly recognisable to a computer programmer.

The scammer may:

- Ask for your credit card details to take a payment for fixing your computer.

- Gain remote access to your computer and download a real virus onto it.

If you give your card details, the scammer will take a considerably larger sum than the reasonable amount he says he is going to charge.

If you fall for this scam, your chances of redress are slim. The scammers tend to operate from abroad. They are therefore difficult for the police to track down and they may anyway be based in a foreign jurisdiction that does not cooperate with the UK police.

Some banks refuse to reimburse victims of this scam, arguing that the victim has given personal details to the scammer and is therefore at fault. Other banks look at this type of fraud on a case-by-case basis.

Even if you do eventually get your money back, it can take a considerable amount of time, especially if you used a debit rather than a credit card.

Things turn nasty

There may be a rather nasty twist to what a caller may claim he can see on your computer. Some victims have been accused of looking at indecent images on the internet.

The caller may actually claim to be a police officer. You are going to be prosecuted and you will be put on the sex offenders register, but you are offered the chance to make a substantial payment to the caller and you won't be reported.

The scammer hopes you will be panicked into paying up whether you have ever looked at pornography or not. As with all blackmailers, one payment will never be enough. If you fall for this once, he will be back demanding more and more.

Take a deep breath. It is not a police officer on the line and he has no idea what is on your computer or what websites you have ever visited. Get whatever details you can about the person who is calling and report him to the police.

The Kiev scam

As with the Lagos scam in Chapter 3, any distant city will do for this scam but the Ukrainian capital of Kiev seems to be favoured. The best choices are somewhere that most people have heard of but are unsure exactly where it is or quite what life there is like – somewhere where there is a perception, rightly or wrongly, that the place sounds a bit like the Wild West.

You receive an email claiming that someone you know is stranded in, let us say, Kiev. They have been robbed of everything apart from the clothes they stand in: their money, credit cards, driving licence, mobile phone, computer and passport have all been taken, so they can't raise money for a ticket home or to get to the British Embassy. They cannot buy food and they are starving.

However, if you transfer money from your bank account to the account detailed in the email your friends will be able to get home and they will repay you promptly on their return.

As with virtually all scams, it needs only one or two people to fall for it and the scammers can make a nice living.

What has happened is that the scammer has succeeded in hacking into your friend's email address book and has sent this message to all the addresses in it.

Just think about it

It needs only a few moments' thought to spot the holes in this farrago of deceit – holes that may not occur to you in your haste to do the decent thing.

What on earth is your friend doing in Kiev? Did they ever mention that they were going? Of course they didn't. They aren't there. A quick phone call to their home or place of work will probably produce a bemused friend wondering what on earth you are on about. Or try ringing their mobile phone. If they answer, it hasn't been stolen!

Here are some questions you may like to consider:

- If your friend's laptop computer has been stolen, how are they managing to get access to their email account to send you a message?

- If all their cash and credit cards have been stolen, how can they use an internet café?
- How can they set up a bank account in a foreign country for you to send money to?
- If all forms of identification have been stolen, how can they prove who they are to draw money out of a bank account?

The simple fact is that if the story were true they would not be able to contact you and you would not be able to get money out to them.

A victim is saved

A friend who is editor of a parish magazine had his email address book hacked and this message was sent out, supposedly from him. An elderly lady rushed round to the home of the parish treasurer asking how she could send money, as she had no idea how to do so.

The treasurer, too, had seen the email. He had also, by chance, seen the supposedly stranded parishioner in the village earlier that morning.

One disadvantage of this scam, from the scammer's point of view, is that the people most likely to fall for it are the least likely to know how to transfer money abroad.

At the time of the incident, Ukraine was in the middle of a civil war as pro-Russian rebels in the east of the country fought to secede to Russia. This surely made it highly unlikely that the person concerned would have ventured there in the first place.

Or perhaps that was part of the scammer's plan. The more urgent the plea seems to be, the more likely it is that someone naïve would be panicked into transferring cash quickly.

Curiosity scams

According to an old proverb, curiosity killed the cat. It can also kill your bank account and your computer.

You receive an intriguing email that puzzles you. It may be notification of a package on its way to you or an invitation to an event. The trouble is, you didn't order anything, nor is it clear who the invitation is from.

Could the message be meant for someone else with a similar email address and it has been sent to you by mistake? This can easily happen, for example, if you have an email address at hotmail.co.uk and someone has an identical address at hotmail.com.

In that case you feel you should do the decent thing and let the sender know. Nor do you want goods coming to you if they are meant for someone else. You could be charged for them or have to go through the rigmarole of sending them back.

Your natural instincts urge caution but your curiosity is aroused. There is a link on the message. Surely there can be no harm in just clicking on it to find out what it's all about, you tell yourself.

Yes, there is harm in doing this. If you are lucky this is just some joker planting a bug on your computer that makes it unusable. The cost of getting an expert to fix it, or even the price of a new computer, is nothing compared to the cost if this is in fact a serious scammer who has planted a Trojan horse bug that transmits details of your bank account or credit cards to him.

The message looks genuine

These messages will usually be dressed up to look genuine. The name of a bona fide courier company may be used, complete with a realistic looking company logo.

One warning sign is that these messages often contain spelling or grammatical errors. The wording of the message can give a clue that the person sending it is not an English speaker and has translated words incorrectly or used phrases that an English speaker would not use.

So if the message has any linguistic errors in it, you can be pretty sure it is a scam.

The message may also contain other slapdash errors, such as letters in different typefaces in the middle of sentences. This is another warning sign of a scam.

However, scammers have become more and more sophisticated and they have generally eliminated the kind of schoolboy errors that alert potential victims, so the fact that an email is in perfect English and is perfectly designed does not guarantee that it is genuine.

The parcel delivery scam

You get an email saying that a delivery firm called when you were out and they need to rearrange the delivery.

You are particularly likely to fall for this scam if you actually are expecting a parcel. Remember that scammers send out messages in bulk. They are just hoping to strike lucky with a small percentage of recipients. Whatever the temptation, do not rush without thinking into clicking on the link provided in the email.

Make a note of the name of the delivery company, which is probably genuine, otherwise you would be less likely to fall for the trick. The delivery company is, however, an innocent bystander. Also note down any reference number provided. This also makes the email look genuine. If there is no reference number you can be sure that the email is a fake.

Close down your emails and use your search engine to find the delivery company's website. Type the reference number into the relevant box on the site. You will soon find out if the delivery is genuine.

Clicking on the link in the email could allow malware to be installed on your computer if this is a scam.

The wedding invitation

Scams often come in batches, then lie dormant for months or years before resurfacing to snare a new generation of victims.

Thus it was that email users received up to half a dozen wedding invitations within a period of a few days. They all looked remarkably similar despite ostensibly coming from different couples.

One other characteristic they had in common was that they gave no indication of who was getting married or where, though some came from a Hong Kong email address.

If someone you know is getting married, surely you would have heard about it. If, despite all odds, it turns out that the invitation was genuine and you missed out on a free feed by not clicking on the link, console yourself with the thought that it could not be anyone close to you.

It's far safer to ask around friends and relations to see if anyone knows of upcoming nuptials.

The summons from Washington

You receive details of a court case in a foreign country. This is the first you have heard of these proceedings and details will be somewhat vague. It is not clear what the case is about or indeed who is suing whom for what.

There will be some kind of deadline, possibly a date set for a hearing or the last day by which you must submit your side of the story.

Scammers will use a legitimate sounding court – indeed it may well be a real court – in a country such as the United States which has a reputation for litigation and a robust legal system that would press for payment of any awards made against you. Washington and New York are favourites for this scam.

The email plays on your fears. What if a case is being brought against you and ignoring the email will mean that you are landed with an enormous legal bill?

Do not reply directly to the email and do not open any attachment under any circumstances. Make a full note of the details – it's all right to print out the contents of the email itself but not an attachment – and use your search engine to find out if the court actually exists.

If it does, the court website may allow you to type in any reference number provided in the email to see if it is genuine. Otherwise email the court explaining the circumstances and ask if you really are named in the case.

You almost certainly won't be, but at least you will have set your mind at rest.

How we can beat the scammers

- Do not take at face value anything a cold caller tells you.

- Do not believe any caller who gives the impression that he works for Microsoft (or any other well-known company) – it doesn't provide that level of personal customer service.

- Remember that cold callers do not know whether your computer has a fault or not – it does not send out signals to remote destinations.

- It's not racist to suspect a cold caller with a heavy foreign accent.

- Do not allow any caller to take control of your computer.

- Be prepared to put the phone down – especially if the caller gets nasty.

- Do not click on links in emails unless you are certain the email is genuine.

- Do not open email attachments unless you are certain they are genuine.

- Do not assume that an email sent from a friend's email address is genuine – their account may have been hacked.

- Do not allow curiosity to get the better of you – if in doubt, delete the email.

Scammers can be remarkably devious and resourceful in finding ways to invade your privacy. Sometimes they go the whole hog and take over your life, as we see in the next chapter.

CHAPTER 22.
The Identity Theft Scam

MANY SCAMS INVOLVE KNOWING SOME OF YOUR personal details but scammers can go one step further and actually take over your whole identity. This may be to steal from you, order goods or run up debts in your name, or simply to pose as you to escape a previous life.

Identity theft is a particularly insidious form of financial scam because you don't know about it until it is far too late. A scammer can take over your identity for some time before you realise it.

It is estimated to cost victims at least £5 million a year, on top of the distress and inconvenience that can be caused.

Unlike conventional email and telephone scams, where you are often alerted by the fact that a complete stranger is contacting you and you have a choice of saying no, identity theft is carried out behind your back and you cannot easily withhold information from the scammers.

You name and address is not a secret. It is on the electoral roll and every envelope you receive. It is probably in the telephone directory. You supply information about your banking arrangements every time you write a cheque.

It is frightening how much information scammers can easily build up:

- Name and address and the length of time you have lived at this address.

- Landline and mobile phone numbers.

- Employers and length of time you have served at each.

- The doctor you are registered with.

This is the sort of information that a bank or business is likely to accept as evidence that the applicant seeking to open a bank account is genuine.

Personal details

As an investigation by the *Daily Mail* discovered, an awful lot of personal information is available and for sale.

Data compiled from health insurance applications is on sale. It contains information on people suffering from diabetes, high blood pressure, osteoporosis, back pain, arthritis and other ailments.

Lists of patients seen by the newspaper included those suffering from deafness, which is of course a group that is particularly vulnerable to scams.

Scammers may know:

- Whether you smoke

- If you want to lose weight

- If you wear glasses or contact lenses

- Your salary
- Ages of your children
- Mortgage details
- Your investment portfolio
- Which credit card you use
- What car you drive
- Details of your insurance policies
- Your mobile network
- Where you buy groceries
- Your hobbies

The *Mail* reported that it had found hundreds of data brokers, including a hypnotherapist, selling private information. It contacted some of the names on the lists for sale and found that the individuals had typically been subject to up to eight calls a day from scammers.

The big advantages for scammers in gaining personal information is that they can:

- Make their pitch sound official
- Target specific audiences
- Keep attacking the victims most likely to give in

One precaution you can take is not to reveal on social media any personal details that might help scammers.

Those who live in flats are particularly vulnerable as scammers can easily gain access to communal areas, where letter boxes are located. Although the boxes are normally locked, with only the resident holding a key to their individual box, it can be possible for a small hand to reach into the slot and extract mail, especially if the box is not emptied regularly and the contents build up, such as when the occupant is on holiday.

When you find out

The first you are likely to hear about your identity being stolen is when you receive bills for goods or services that you haven't ordered.

You may receive a letter from a bank saying that you have been declined for a loan. This is a piece of luck, as the scammer has been a little too greedy and you are alerted to the scam before your money has been stolen.

Particularly unpleasant is to find that someone has managed to obtain a loan from a payday lender that starts to extract large sums from your bank account.

It is very important to act swiftly to limit the damage. Contact your own bank immediately when you suspect foul play to see if unauthorised payments have been made since you last checked your bank statement. Alert any supplier who sends unsolicited goods, although these are more likely to go to a different address from your own.

If you hear you have been declined a loan you never applied for, contact the company concerned to let them know. Then if the scammer reapplies for a smaller amount this will not be granted.

Credit rating agencies

If you suspect someone may have stolen or used your identity, check with a credit rating agency such as Experian or Equifax. There is only a nominal fee for this routine service and it's well worth the expense to find out if other loans have been applied for in your name. Lenders will typically check with these agencies to see if you have any black marks against your name, such as unpaid debts or county court judgements.

Contact any bank that has inquired about your credit rating and if necessary be persistent to ensure that loans are not granted in your name. It is much easier to prevent a fraudulent loan in advance than it is to unpick one that has been granted and paid out.

You can pay a monthly fee to the credit agencies to be alerted to any applications made in your name.

For £12 a year you can join fraud protection agency Cifas (www.cifas.org.uk), a not-for-profit membership association representing the private and public sectors. It was originally called Credit Industry Fraud Avoidance Service but has dropped the full name because it has widened its service.

Another step to take if you suspect foul play is to contact your doctor, especially if you are receiving medical treatment. Identity thieves have been known to switch the NHS registration to another GP.

How we can beat the scammers

- Shred any piece of paper that has your name and address on it before you bin it.

- Shred any bills or other official paperwork so the scammer is unable to gain vital clues about what services you use.

- Limit the information you put on social media or, better still, keep all your personal details secret.

- Act swiftly if you suspect you have had your identity stolen – don't just hope for the best.

So far we have concentrated on scams that affect individuals. However, in some ways we are more vulnerable in the workplace, where we tend to be complacent, thinking that scams are for our employer to worry about. In the following chapter we consider why we should not jeopardise our jobs by making our workplace our weakspot.

CHAPTER 23.
Company Scams

U NFORTUNATELY CRIMINALS USE SOME OF THEIR ILL-gotten gains to devise ever more sophisticated scams, such as one uncovered by technology group IBM in which a well-funded Eastern European gang of cyber criminals used a combination of phishing, malware and phone calls to steal more than $1 billion from large and medium-sized US companies.

The Dyre Wolf

The scheme, dubbed The Dyre Wolf by the IBM researchers who uncovered it, targeted people working in companies by sending spam emails with unsafe attachments that installed a variant of existing malware known as Dyre onto as many computers as possible.

The malware waits until it recognises that the user is navigating to a bank website and instantly creates a fake screen telling the user that the bank's site is having problems. The user is told to call a telephone number that the user mistakenly believes belongs to their bank.

In fact, the call puts them through to an English-speaking operator who already knows what bank the users think they are contacting.

The operator then asks for the users' banking details and immediately starts a large transfer to take money out of the relevant account.

Once the transfer is complete, the money is then quickly moved from bank to bank to evade detection. In one instance, IBM said, the gang hit the victim company with what is known as a denial of service attack – in layman's terms, crashing the company's computers – so it would not discover the theft until much later.

The imitation game

Further proof that even corporate finance professionals can get caught in expensive scams was provided when a company based in Omaha, Nebraska, lost a total of $17.2 million in an email fraud.

The emails were sent to Keith McMurtry, the corporate controller at Scoular, a privately owned commodities trader founded 120 years ago. They appeared to have come from Chuck Elsea, the chief executive, and from the company's auditing firm. The fraudsters used email addresses set up in Germany, France and Israel and servers located in Moscow.

The FBI said that the first email told McMurtry to transfer $780,000 to Shanghai Pudong Development Bank – a genuine institution. The following day he complied with another instruction to transfer $7 million, and then he sent another $9.4 million three days later.

The fact that the emails were sent from a different address than the one usually used by Elsea failed to arouse the suspicions of the financial controller. The first two emails from Elsea's fake address stated that the transfers were for an unpublicised acquisition of a Chinese company and swore his colleague to secrecy.

Scoular had been considering expanding in China but it is not known whether the fraudsters knew this or just struck lucky. Persuading victims not to mention the transaction to other people is a popular trick played by scammers.

The second email gave the arrangement an air of legitimacy by telling McMurtry to contact an employee of the auditing firm for details of where to send the funds.

He subsequently received an email that appeared to be from the auditing firm telling him to send the money to the Chinese bank. This email seemed to be genuine and it gave a phone number that McMurtry called. The person who answered gave his name and it matched a name mentioned in the email.

Insurance is not the full answer

It does seem that companies have become more conscious of falling victim to scams, which is perhaps a reflection of how many have been caught out.

Lloyd's of London, one of the world's largest insurance markets, reported a 50% increase in premiums for insurance against cyber attacks in the first quarter of 2015 compared with the same three months of 2014.

About 70% of the extra premiums came from first-time customers but Lloyd's also reported that existing customers were raising their level of cover. Figures from the UK Cabinet

Office suggested that 81% of large business and 60% of small businesses now suffered a cyber security breach each year.

Lloyd's covers more than 10% of the global cyber insurance market and its experience is reflected around the world. An insurance industry report said that global premium income from cyber insurance rose 50% in 2014 to about £2 billion.

However, insuring against an attack adds to the cost of doing business and it is no substitute for taking stringent measures to prevent attacks in the first place.

Register scams

A register scam targets businesses but can also be directed at any individual who is self-employed.

The scammers pose as publishers of magazines, directories or website registration companies. Victims have reported being sent invoices to 'renew' their internet domain name at a very high cost.

Getting your company name circulated among potential new customers can be particularly tempting for small businesses in niche markets.

Alas, these directories may be non-existent. At best they are likely to be of very limited use. Ask yourself, do you read directories of companies? Neither do other people. Nor have you any idea whether the directories will be circulated widely or whether they will be targeted at companies and people who are likely to want your services.

This type of scammer tends to be particularly persistent. The number of people who might want to be in a directory is comparatively limited so the scammer has to make the most of what opportunities there are.

Only the lowly

This scam is aimed at people who are very busy and are likely to say yes just to get the scammer off their back. Alternatively, the target may be someone quite low in an organisation who can be flattered and bamboozled. Scammers can be very charming.

Lowly employees who sign up to something they shouldn't have done are likely to panic and try to cover their tracks, so there is greater scope for repeat invoices. The victim is reluctant to admit openly to having wasted the firm's money.

Even where no authorisation has been given, the scammers will send invoices in the hope that they get paid by mistake. They may produce a copy of the directory, if it actually exists, as proof they are entitled to payment.

An extension of the register scam is for unethical suppliers to trick employees into signing for goods such as stationery that are fairly inexpensive. Employees find themselves agreeing to purchase ever-increasing quantities of little-used products. Again, the employee may be pressured into hiding the blunder for fear of getting the sack.

Surveys

An alternative to register scams is for the scammer to contact victims pretending to be conducting a survey.

People are generally reluctant to put the phone down or slam the door on a caller as it could be a genuine survey that helps to make some aspect of life better. It seems mean to be rude to someone who is probably not well paid and is trying to do an honest day's work. You can ask for identification and which company they work for but this is little by way of a safeguard. Even the dubious ones will have name tags dangling from their necks.

You think there is little harm in taking part, as you are being asked to provide answers to questions, not hand over cash.

Unfortunately, as often with scams, you have no way of knowing whether a survey is genuine or a trick. You may find yourself giving out lots of information about your business that helps a scammer to target it.

If it is not a genuine survey, you may end up on the receiving end of a hard sell. The caller will try to make an appointment for a salesperson to visit you. Don't feel obliged to roll over; terminate conversations with pushy salespeople immediately.

How we can beat the scammers

There are simple steps you can take to minimize the risk:

- Take care when paying any invoice or transferring company money. Are you sending it where you think you are?

- Never sign up to join a business directory you haven't heard of.

- If you do choose to advertise in a directory, make sure that it is limited to one edition and is not open-ended.

- Don't let a complete stranger take control of your advertising decisions.

- All orders, however small, should be recorded with, and authorised by, the person who deals with accounts.

- If you are conned as an employee, own up immediately and limit the damage.

- If the scammer claims that there is an ongoing contract, ask to see it. At least you will find out whether you are really contracted to pay anything and who authorised the payments in the first place.

- As with all cold calls, simply put the phone down if you feel uncomfortable.

- Don't be lulled into agreeing to anything – ask for time to think about it.

- If your reticence provokes anger or aggression in the caller, don't be bullied.

TOP TIPS

If you are targeted in a scam

I F YOU HAVE BEEN TARGETED BY A SCAM, OR KNOW SOMEONE who has been, call Action Fraud, the UK's national reporting centre for fraud and internet crime on 0300 123 2040, or visit its website: www.actionfraud.police.uk

If credit or debit cards, online banking or cheques are involved in the scam your first step should be to contact your bank or credit card company. If your bank refuses to refund money taken fraudulently, you have the right to appeal to the Financial Ombudsman Service.

If you think something may be a scam, phone the Citizens Advice Consumer Service on 08454 040506. They pass details of the case on to Trading Standards officers if appropriate. The Trading Standards service is responsible for protecting consumers and the community against rogue traders.

Above all, warn family, friends, neighbours, the local Neighbourhood Watch scheme and anyone else who will listen. Tweet about it. If you have been conned, at least you can save other people from the same fate.

The best policy is to avoid becoming a victim in the first place. Follow these tips:

- Never do business with someone who makes an unsolicited approach to you. If you want a job done, find someone you trust to do it.

- Don't do business on your front doorstep.

- Put the phone down on cold callers. Don't worry about being rude. They are the ones invading your space.

- Don't sound interested in anything a cold caller tells you. It only encourages them.

- Never press a button on your telephone keypad when prompted to do so by a cold call.

- Do not allow a cold caller remote access to your computer.

- Never click on a link in an email unless you are absolutely certain it is genuine. If you have the slightest doubt, check with the sender, and even then you should click on it only if you know the sender.

- Log directly onto webpages rather than gaining access through links in emails.

- Never hand over your credit or debit card to a stranger. If you use it to pay a bill in a shop or restaurant, do not let it out of your sight.

- Never divulge any password – credit card, online banking, computer access – to anyone. Your password is intended to stop anyone posing as you.

- Never divulge any PINs. These are effectively passwords.

- Always check monthly statements such as those for bank accounts or store cards as soon as you receive them to see if there are any items you don't recognise. If there are, raise a query immediately. It doesn't matter if it turns out to be a genuine item.

- Don't allow yourself to be panicked into taking hasty action.

- Do not respond to offers to remove yourself from a database by pressing a button on your telephone.

- Do not click any links in dubious-looking junk mail, including those that supposedly remove you from a database of recipients. Just delete the email.

- If you buy anything online, do not agree to an unusual payment method. Better to miss out on your cherished purchase than have a crook disappear with your money.

- If you think that you are the target of a scam, phone Action Fraud, the national reporting centre for fraud and internet crime, on 0300 123 2040 to report it.

- Remember above all else: if it looks too good to be true, it's a scam.

*   *   *

I hope this book has helped to draw your attention to the many ways scammers and fraudsters operate, and that it may prevent you from being a victim of one of these scams in the future.

Keep vigilant and stay safe out there.

APPENDIX

Useful phone numbers and websites

Action Fraud

The UK's fraud and crime reporting centre.
Phone: 0300 123 2040
www.actionfraud.police.uk

Cifas

A not-for-profit fraud prevention service representing the private and public sectors.
www.cifas.org.uk

The Insurance Fraud Bureau Cheatline

A not-for-profit company established in 2006 to lead the insurance industry's fight against insurance fraud.
Phone: 0800 422 0421
www.insurancefraudbureau.org

The Pensions Regulator

The UK regulator of work-based pension schemes
www.thepensionsregulator.gov.uk/pension-scams

Citizens Advice Consumer Service

Advice on consumer issues, energy supply and postal service.
Phone: 08454 040506
www.gov.uk/citizens-advice-consumer-service

Credit rating checks

Experian: www.experian.co.uk
Equifax: www.equifax.co.uk

Solicitors Regulation Authority (England and Wales)

Regulates solicitors and protects consumers.
Phone: 0370 606 2555
Email: contactcentre@sra.org.uk
www.sra.org.uk

The Law Society of Scotland

The professional body for Scotish solicitors.
Phone: 0131 226 7411
www.lawscot.org.uk

The Financial Ombudsman Service

Investigates consmer financial complaints.
Phone: 0800 023 4 567
www.financial-ombudsman.org.uk

THANKS
FOR READING!

Our readers mean everything to us at Harriman House. As a special thank you for buying this book, let us help you save as much as possible on your next read:

If you've never ordered from us before, get £5 off your first order at **harriman-house.com** with this code: bos51

Already a customer? Get £5 off an order of £25 or more with this code: bos25

Get 7 days' FREE access to hundreds of our books at **volow.co** – simply head to the website and sign up.

Thanks again!
from the team at

Codes can only be used once per customer and order. T&Cs apply.

Lightning Source UK Ltd.
Milton Keynes UK
UKOW06f2219240216

269025UK00010B/162/P

9 780857 194862